Praise for
On the Road With the ḷ

Testimonies are more than good stories. In essence, they declare and prophesy what God wants to do again. In doing so, they reveal the heart of a loving Father who longs to partner with us for His glory to be seen in the earth. Ken Fish, in his new book, *On the Road With the Holy Spirit*, brilliantly and simply unpacks five essential values of the Christian life. Each chapter ends with amazing God stories that illustrate and establish the truths talked about. I joyfully endorse both the man and his message. This book is certain to encourage each reader for a life of great impact.

—BILL JOHNSON
SENIOR LEADER, BETHEL CHURCH

My good friend Ken Fish tells stories of the supernatural that often seem unbelievable. But they are always true and always point us to Jesus, who is the author of the miracles. I hope this astonishing collection of stories from Ken's ministry life will provoke every reader to jealousy—which is to say I hope we will all pray to experience similar things and to see what the living God can do in our own lives to His eternal glory. This is a vitally important book.

—ERIC METAXAS
NEW YORK TIMES BEST-SELLING AUTHOR;
HOST, *THE ERIC METAXAS RADIO SHOW*

On the Road With the Holy Spirit is an inspiring, faith-building read. It is not the product of an armchair theologian but of an itinerant teacher of the ways of God. Ken Fish is primarily an equipper of the saints, and in doing so, he provides a strong biblical basis for his practices and teachings. I recommend Ken's new book to all who want to be better equipped in the Spirit and by the Word of God to do the deeds of God through the power of God's Spirit.

—RANDY CLARK, DMIN
FOUNDER, GLOBAL AWAKENING

Ken Fish consistently ministers in more miraculous power than anyone I know. Though some readers may find it difficult to believe some of the stories in this book, I know Ken to be a teller of the truth. This book has the potential to help you experience similar miracles in your life and ministry and to hear God's voice better.

—JACK DEERE
AUTHOR, *SURPRISED BY THE POWER OF THE SPIRIT*

For over forty years, Ken Fish has been used by the Holy Spirit to pray for the sick and minister to people in powerful ways. He has also been a zealous student of the Scriptures with an observable love for Jesus and people. His accounts of what he has learned provide both inspiration as well as practical ways to equip others to minister in the Holy Spirit.

—MIKE BICKLE
FOUNDER, INTERNATIONAL HOUSE OF PRAYER
OF KANSAS CITY

If you are hungry for supernatural adventures with God, this book is for you. It is filled with page after page of incredible insight and testimonies of extraordinary deliverances and notable miracles. Ken Fish makes the point throughout that these kinds of amazing manifestations are for you too!

—CINDY JACOBS
COFOUNDER, GENERALS INTERNATIONAL

In every generation, God raises up forerunners of the faith who run hard after the Holy Spirit, paving the way for others who will stand on their shoulders. Ken Fish, author, international spokesman, and healing ambassador, shows that signs and wonders are for today. A new global generation is truly arising in Christ Jesus. And signs and wonders are your keys to writing your own diary of the supernatural!

—JAMES W. GOLL
FOUNDER, GOD ENCOUNTERS MINISTRIES

What sets this book apart from most contemporary testimonies of the supernatural is a rich matrix of theological, historical, and cultural insights. This "diary of signs and wonders" invites readers on a five-year spiritual pilgrimage through continents, cultures, languages, and religions. The message is clear: Christ's transforming presence and power are available to anyone, anywhere, anytime. Organized around five pillars—prophetic ministry, purity, power, God's presence, and prayer—this is no ordinary book. Solid theological foundations require deep reading that transforms the mind, which is what you'll get when you walk the road with Ken Fish.

—KEVIN SPRINGER
COAUTHOR, *POWER EVANGELISM*

ON THE ROAD
with the *Holy Spirit*

KEN FISH

publisher nor the author assumes any responsibility for errors or for changes that occur after publication. Further, the publisher does not have any control over and does not assume any responsibility for author or third-party websites or their content.

For more Spirit-led resources, visit charismahouse.com and the author's website at orbisministries.org.

Cataloging-in-Publication Data is on file with the Library of Congress.
International Standard Book Number: 978-1-63641-254-2
E-book ISBN: 978-1-63641-255-9

23 24 25 26 27 — 987654321
Printed in the United States of America

Most Charisma Media products are available at special quantity discounts for bulk purchase for sales promotions, premiums, fund-raising, and educational needs. For details, call us at (407) 333-0600 or visit our website at www.charismamedia.com.

Dedication

THIS BOOK IS dedicated to many. First, I dedicate it to my wife, Beth, and to my children, Rebekah, Anastasia, and Charissa. Without your patience and hunger for the Lord, it would never have been written. We learned many of these truths together. Additionally, you allowed me to travel and be on the road with the Holy Spirit so I could learn in depth about all that I have written here.

Next, I also dedicate this book to those who have taught me about the ways of the Holy Spirit. First among these were my grandparents John and Dorothy Wolbert, who taught me the Bible in my childhood and who influenced me in my youth and beyond. Their training developed in me a lifelong hunger for the supernatural aspects of the Christian faith. I would not be who I am were it not for their influence.

In addition to my grandparents, I would be remiss if I didn't include John Wimber, who taught me so many of the foundational truths that led to the experiences recounted herein. Among these were an understanding of the kingdom of heaven and of healing. I don't think I would have had these experiences without my relationship with John and the training I received from him. Today, Randy Clark and Bill Johnson carry forward the groundbreaking work and the mentorship that John was doing forty years ago. Additionally, Blaine and Becky Cook allowed me to observe and learn from them in so many ways and different situations that I can't even recall all of them now. If John Wimber laid the foundation as a wise master builder, the Cooks provided the finished carpentry work. I also want to give special mention to Lonnie Frisbee, whom I met at the Vineyard Anaheim and with whom

I was a fellow traveler for a season. He taught me many things about the power of the Holy Spirit and about the negative power of the human soul. Also from this season of my life, Kevin and Suzanne Springer taught me many of the principles of Christian character and discipleship that continue to guide and ground my life.

The influence of Mike Bickle and the Kansas City Prophets, especially Bob Jones, John Paul Jackson, and James Goll, has also been profound but in a very different way from those I've named previously. Through the Vineyard, I learned about worship, compassion, and power. Through these men from Kansas City, I learned about intercession and the prophetic dimensions of the Spirit that open the way to understanding the mind and the ways of the Lord. Although not from Kansas City, both Jack Deere and Cindy Jacobs provided finishing touches to this training. They built a bridge between all that I learned from the Vineyard and all that I learned from Kansas City Fellowship, now known as the International House of Prayer of Kansas City.

Finally, I dedicate this book to the Lord Jesus Christ, who saved me from my sins when I was young and rescued me from many of the trials and perils of life before they could overtake me. He invited me on an adventure that has not yet ended. He is the same yesterday, today, and forever, and He is the one who ultimately has made all of what I have written possible by His Spirit. Additionally, as amazing as this journey has been, it is merely a foretaste of what awaits those who follow Him when we will all see Him face to face.

> We are like dwarfs sitting on the shoulders of giants. We see more, and things that are more distant, than they did, not because our sight is superior or because we are taller than they, but because they raise us up, and by their great stature add to ours.
> —JOHN OF SALISBURY, *THE METALOGICON*, AD 1159

Contents

Foreword

ANYONE ENGAGED IN extensive international travel, particularly to some of the less economically developed locations where Ken Fish has traveled, will recognize the physical demands such travel exacts on the body. This book illustrates, however, the extensive ways the Lord has blessed Ken's sacrifices for the kingdom.

Ken's compassion for the broken pervades his narrative, and I have witnessed how he sacrifices his time and rest in seeking people's healing and deliverance. He is honest when healings are incomplete, yet he also anguishes on people's behalf. He does not give up easily but continues to look for ways to bring their healing, which they often experience. In our world of division, Ken's further commitment to and voice for interdenominational unity in the gospel is refreshing.

His kingdom theology brings together Word and Spirit and invites signs of the kingdom that honor our King in this age as well as in the coming one. Some of the exorcism accounts challenge my theology and invite me to search the Scriptures afresh with questions I have not considered. This is not to say that I or every other reader will interpret every experience in this book in the same way; it is to say that these are firsthand accounts, recorded while fresh in the author's mind, and that readers must therefore take them into account.

Such accounts can challenge some of our prior expectations based on lack of experience. On one occasion I was present when Ken taught for several days about the ministry of deliverance. Afterward, he and others began demonstrating in practice what he had just taught, and I witnessed a demonized person's body contorting in ways I had not deemed humanly possible until the person was ultimately set free. On other occasions I have interviewed people healed from medically reported disabilities when Ken or his colleagues prayed for them.

Because this book treats only a limited period in Ken's ministry, it necessarily omits some of my favorite accounts, which include some even more dramatic and fascinating than most in this book. Nevertheless, what it does include is plenty dramatic enough to keep us turning the pages and, more importantly, enough to challenge us to greater faith.

Meanwhile, don't skip the appendixes, which contain some particularly important insights, especially for putting into practice the principles illustrated earlier in the book.

Accounts that exceed my own experience are good to stretch my faith. This book invites a higher level of expectation in the best sense: not telling God what to do but recognizing and embracing God working in our midst, maintaining readiness to pray and keep praying, and continuing to look to God as if He is—because He is—still the living God of Scripture.

—Craig Keener, PhD
F. M. and Ada Thompson Professor of Biblical Studies,
Asbury Theological Seminary

Acknowledgments

BOOKS ARE A collaborative effort between those who inspired the author, the author himself or herself, and those who assist the author in rendering the final version of the book. In addition to those mentioned in my dedication, I want to acknowledge those who helped birth this book.

I acknowledge Russell Bratton, who helped me a great deal when the Australian Outpouring was just getting started. He was the first one to encourage me to keep a journal of my experiences. Were it not for that word of encouragement, I would not have had the records with which to write this book.

My friend from Princeton, Linda Francese Falter, deserves special mention for poring over those journals and selecting with an editor's eye some of the most compelling and relevant entries. Unfortunately, many more entries were left "on the cutting room floor."

The final editing work was assisted by Karla Dial. She has a keen eye for detail and good command of English grammar and syntax. I would not have met Karla were it not for Eric Metaxas, who deserves special mention.

Finally, I want to acknowledge Stephen and Joy Strang for their friendship and support of this project.

Thank you, all of you, for your friendship and help.

Introduction

I HAVE BEEN FASCINATED with the supernatural acts of God since childhood. I remember hearing stories from the Bible from my grandmother and grandfather and thinking, "I want to do that!" Whenever I would ask my grandparents about such things, they would say, "Oh, those things don't happen anymore"— but my hunger persisted.

Late in high school, I had a supernatural encounter with God that altered my life forever. From there I went off to college, where I became even hungrier to experience God as those who lived in biblical times did.

While I was in college, I was introduced to the teachings of John Wimber and subsequently had the good fortune of not only meeting but also working for him. These events set the trajectory of my life and forever altered my understanding of the veracity of Scripture. As time went on, I learned that the accounts of miraculous acts of God in the Bible were, in fact, true because I saw them happening around me—and later through my own ministry.

Beginning in 2010, the Lord opened a new chapter in my journey with Him. I left my twenty-five-year career as an executive at Fortune 500 companies and began traveling and teaching the things that I had learned and experienced of God throughout my life. These travels took me to more than forty-five nations, where I experienced all manner of miracles and healings (which, by the way, are not always the same); as a result, I can now say I have seen nearly every miracle described in the Bible with my own eyes.

This book is a travelogue blended with theological insights and reflections. I have selected key events from those years and have attempted to explain how they occurred through a theological lens that I consider to include five key pillars to a life of the miraculous: prophetic ministry, purity, power, presence, and prayer.

Signs and wonders are real, but they do not occur in a vacuum. Our Father has ordered the universe in such a way that certain things don't happen unless other things happen first. What I am calling the five pillars are really a matrix into which the life of signs and wonders must be set. If these things are absent, signs and wonders will inevitably fail to occur or decline until they occur no more. To use the language of formal logic, they are a necessary, but insufficient, condition to embark upon a life of the miraculous. To some, they will seem elementary; to others, legalistic; to still others, revelatory. Not everyone understands these five factors in the same way, so I will explain them in greater detail at key junctures throughout the book. Here is a brief summary:

- The prophetic voice of God is active communication from God to humanity expressed in a local context with an intended outcome. That is to say, our Father interacts with His people in two-way dialogue, much as we understand from reading Scripture at face value. For some people, this is a shocking idea and one they have never encountered personally. Others may have a theological presupposition that God no longer interacts with the world in this way (and perhaps never has). Of course, if we understand that God is our Father and He can speak, then it should be axiomatic that when He speaks, we obey, and quickly. So when we speak of the prophetic being a pillar of living a life of signs and wonders, I am saying that we rely—moment by moment, day by day, and week by week—on two-way communication with our

Father. Without this, a life of signs and wonders is not possible.

- Purity is difficult to discuss in today's society because we have been trained both by precept and example to recoil from the concept of holiness. Often we confuse holiness with sanctimoniousness. Holiness is an internal matter that flows out of our union with Jesus, but it is not just a concept; it must practically flow out into our lives. Holy people understand that they are cleansed by the Holy Spirit. Our Father does not make His home with those who do not live by His ways. He has commanded us to be holy as He is holy (1 Pet. 1:16). So when we speak of purity, we speak of a particular kind of scruple in which we dare not violate the standards of our Father despite what the desires of our own flesh or the standards of the people among whom we live may be. We do this not because we seek to earn anything from our Father but out of deference to Him and His stated preferences about our attitudes, speech, and lifestyle.

- Power is the dynamic, active power of God released into a situation. In this instance, power is more than inspiration and more than the sense of powerful speech that we often encounter in religious meetings whereby one might say, "That sermon was powerful!" God's power is dynamic, active, and tangible so that when it is loosed in our midst, things change. It literally flows out of the being of God Himself and often causes things that could not happen to occur. In the Gospel of

Luke, we read the story of a woman who had been bleeding for twelve years; when she touched the hem of Jesus' garment, He felt power flow out of His body and she was instantly healed. To live a supernatural life means that the power of God is around us and at times flows through us, just as it did through Jesus.

- Presence is the omnipresence of God, sometimes called His ubiquity. That is to say, God is everywhere, but we don't always experience this tangibly. For example, Jacob awoke from a dream in which he saw a ladder, and he said, "Surely the LORD is in this place, and I did not know it" (Gen. 28:16). When we speak of God's presence in this sense, we are speaking of the conscious presence of God Himself around us and inside us. This allows us to enjoy Him and teaches us a healthy fear of the Lord and a reverence for His precepts. Importantly, it includes both the understanding and lived reality that wherever we go, we carry the presence of God, creating an opening for Him to move in a particular situation. Thus, "presence" in this sense carries the understanding that we can discern when the Lord is ready to move on a person, in a church, or over a region (cf. Luke 5:17).

- All religious traditions contain the common thread of prayer, though what that prayer entails varies from one tradition to another. One of the most important pictures of prayer the Bible paints for us is that when we pray, we are speaking with our Father. He hears us, and because He has heard us, He answers us. But this is not the lived reality of many Christians. Additionally, prayer can function in multiple dimensions. At times it has to do with intercession, whereby we call upon God to move in a particular area or time with an expected outcome. Other times it has to do with contemplation or adoration. This prayer is—in the language of another era—supplication, to ask humbly while nevertheless expecting to receive. Jesus, the apostles, and most of the prophets knew what it was to pray in confident expectation that God would answer their prayers affirmatively. So we are to approach God in confident expectation of what He will do not because we are good, but because He is good. We approach not because we are wise, but because we pray according to His will, principally revealed through His Word and also prophetically. The life of prayer that gives rise to a life of miracles is first of all one of intercession, which bathes the context in petitions for God's intervention. Second, it requests that God intervene in a specific situation and interval of time in a way that far transcends humans' ability to manipulate the outcome in a particular way and time frame.

The stories in this book are only a small sampling of the many I have seen; the time interval I have selected is based on journals I was keeping at the time. I could have chosen a period before 2010 or between 2010 and 2022. Had I done so, the stories would have changed, but their nature would not. Some of these stories may amaze or shock you, but I have selected them all with the intent to testify to the works of our Father and to illustrate the framework of the five pillars on which this book focuses.

What I have learned from all of this is that God is not a theory. His Word is true, and the things described in the Bible continue today for those who are willing to embrace the ways of the Holy Spirit while following in the footsteps of Jesus. I do not consider myself to be exceptional but rather one of those who believe. And as the Scripture says, "These signs *will* accompany those who believe" (Mark 16:17, emphasis added).

Christianity is more than a religion. It is more than a belief system. It is more than a worldview. It is an invitation to go on an adventure with our Father, both in this life and into eternity. I pray that this book will kindle a hunger in your heart to join that adventure and to experience a life—and a lifestyle—marked by signs and wonders.

—Ken Fish
December 2022

PILLAR 1

Prophetic Ministry

And he will turn the hearts of fathers to their children and the hearts of children to their fathers, lest I come and strike the land with a decree of utter destruction.

—MALACHI 4:6

And he will turn many of the children of Israel to the LORD their God, and he will go before him in the spirit and power of Elijah, to turn the hearts of the fathers to the children, and the disobedient to the wisdom of the just, to make ready for the LORD a people prepared.

—LUKE 1:16–17

THE WORDS OF Malachi are the last spoken words of God until the dawn of the New Testament era, approximately four hundred years later. It is noteworthy that the New Testament opens with a citation of the Old Testament's closing words. It is even more significant that both passages speak of a future reconciliation between the "fathers" (i.e., those who have gone before us) and the "children" of the current generation back to the wisdom and ways of those who preceded them. I do not mean literal fathers and their earthly children (although this passage could apply to them as well). Instead, the clear implication of both passages is that there has been a significant breach between the fathers of the faith and the children of their spiritual legacy. This state of affairs has resurfaced in our present day between the fathers—sometimes called the "great cloud of witnesses" (Heb. 12:1, MEV)—and the children of this present generation, who are, in fact, modern believers of all ages and denominational affiliations. The results of this breach are many. And the cause? A woeful ignorance of Scripture and an even more woeful ignorance of church history.

Everywhere I go, I see and hear this ignorance. It is reflected in what preachers say and in what people believe. On the one hand, these two disjunctions cause the children of this generation to reject things that other generations of the church would have readily accepted. This includes doctrine and practice. On the other hand, these disjunctions also cause the children of this generation to accept things that other generations of the church would have viewed with suspicion or dismissed out of hand. Let's look at two examples, two currently emerging trends within the Charismatic/Spirit-filled church: Gnosticism and the rejection of the authority of Scripture. Movements within Christianity have come and gone since the beginning, some beneficial and some destructive. The point: without a strong knowledge of Scripture and church history, we may fail miserably to know the difference.

In AD 144 the Roman church excommunicated a man named Marcion. Born the son of a bishop in AD 85, Marcion had been a wealthy shipping magnate in Sinope, Turkey, but had come to Rome in the aftermath of the Bar-Kochba Revolt/War (AD 132–136) between the Romans and the Jews. This conflict displaced many in the Eastern Mediterranean. Marcion believed that Jesus was the Savior sent by God and that Paul was His chief apostle.

But Marcion also seems to have held some Gnostic beliefs: Among several distinctive teachings, he rejected the validity of the Hebrew Bible and its God along with most of the New Testament, other than the synoptic gospels and the writings of Paul. Marcionites believed the Hebrew God was full of wrath and a separate, lesser entity than the forgiving God of the New Testament. Marcion's canon consisted of just eleven books: ten passages from Luke's Gospel and ten letters of Paul. All other

Epistles and Gospels in the twenty-seven-book New Testament are absent from Marcion's canon. The ten selected Epistles of Paul enjoy prominence in Marcion's canon, since Marcion credits Paul alone with accurately communicating the universality of Jesus' message of love, grace, and acceptance. After his excommunication, Marcion started his own movement of churches that persisted well beyond his death in AD 160. For over three hundred years, until well into the time of the Byzantine Empire, his works were widely read, leading opponents to denounce Marcionism as heresy. Most notably, Tertullian wrote a five-book treatise titled *Adversus Marcionem* (*Against Marcion*) around AD 208.

If the teachings of Marcion sound vaguely familiar, they should. From time to time his distinctive emphases have periodically resurfaced. Each time the church has universally decried these teachings as heretical, yet many of Marcion's teachings appear to be coming to the fore again in the hyper-grace movement. To be fair, not all hyper-grace teachers say exactly the same things as Marcion (or as each other, for that matter), but similarities exist between many of their teachings and those of Marcion. For example, the widely touted statements that the Old Testament no longer matters and that there can be few to no moral strictures placed on believers because "we aren't under law but under grace" are two problematic teachings that fit within the Marcionite framework. "Turning back to the fathers" suggests that we at least consider this new emphasis in the light of all that the ancients have previously written.

The other emerging trend is akin to ancient Gnosticism, though not identical. By its very nature, Gnosticism is fluid and subject to change based on the specific context despite certain common themes. Gnostic ideas influenced many ancient religions, but they especially impacted early Christianity with the notion "that *gnosis* (variously interpreted as knowledge, enlightenment, salvation, emancipation [freedom] or 'oneness with God') may be reached by practicing philanthropy to the point of personal poverty, [practicing] sexual abstinence (as far as possible for hearers and completely for initiates) and diligently searching for wisdom" through a life of service.[1] At times these and other practices may have looked similar to Orthodox Christian practices or even overlapped entirely. For example, Gnostic practices such as prolonged fasting, times of extended prayer, and ecstatic worship were also known to be Christian practices, which made discernment both difficult and imperative. This is why John's Gospel has a decidedly different tone and focus than those of Matthew, Mark, and Luke. Finally, many scholars think parts of Romans, Galatians, and 1 Thessalonians are also intended to refute the early threads of this kind of teaching.

In Gnosticism, the lower world is broadly associated with matter and time and more particularly with a fleshly, imperfect, transient world. The upper world is associated with the world of God, the soul, and perfection. The soul is expected to rise (or ascend) into God and His eternal, nonphysical world (similar to the current and growing emphasis on the third heaven). To ascend to God, the Gnostic apprehends specific, hidden knowledge that mixes philosophy, metaphysics, the secrets of history, and the secrets of the universe. These may also be mixed with natural curiosity, culture, and knowledge. Nearly all mystery religions and secret societies (like the Freemasons, and in particular the Rosicrucians as a branch of Freemasonry) traffic in these same categories.

Other distinctive ancient Gnostic emphases include the following:

- "the notion of a [possibly] remote, supreme, monadic divinity [or] source." This figure is the totality of the divine powers and emanations and is "known by a variety of names, including 'Pleroma' (fullness, totality) and 'Bythos' (depth, profundity)."[2]

- "the introduction by emanation of further divine [or spiritual] beings known as Aeons." These aeons seek to reunite with the one source, being aspects of the God from which they proceeded—broken off, as it were, to embed in the individual. The "emanations are often conceived metaphorically as a gradual and progressive distancing from the ultimate source, which brings about an instability in the fabric of the divine nature" of the spiritual universe.[3]

- the existence of "a distinct creator god or demiurge, which is an illusion [or possibly] a later emanation from the single monad or source." This creator god is inferior to the source, and as master over the material world it is a lesser or false god, antagonistic to the spiritual world. This secondary god is commonly referred to as the *demiourgós* described in the writings of Plato (fourth century BC) and the philosophical and theological traditions that follow him. The Gnostic demiurge resembles figures in Plato's *Timaeus* and *The Republic*. "The relevant passage of *The Republic* was found within a major Gnostic library discovered at Nag Hammadi, wherein a text existed describing the demiurge as a 'lion-faced serpent.' Elsewhere this figure is called 'Ialdabaoth' [or Yaldabaoth], 'Samael' (Aramaic: *sæm'a-'el*, or 'blind god'), or 'Saklas' (Syriac: *sækla*, 'the foolish one')," Ahriman, El, Satan, and even Yahweh. The demiurge is "sometimes ignorant of the superior god" and sometimes malevolent (hence the attribution in at least some sources of the name Satan). "The demiurge typically creates [or recruits] a group of co-actors named [*archa* (singular: *archon*; see Ephesians 6:12)], who preside over the material realm and, in some cases, present obstacles to the soul seeking ascent from it."[4]

- an "estimation of the world, owing to [that just mentioned], as flawed or a production of 'error' but possibly good [redeemable]" if its constituents will allow this. This world is typically seen as an inferior representation of "a higher-level reality or consciousness" just as a model of an object would be inferior to the object itself. In more extreme cases, the Gnostic view of materiality takes on the ascetic tendency to view the human body as evil and constrictive, thus the world becomes a "prison for its inhabitants. The explanation of this state... [lies] in the use of a complex mythological-cosmological drama in which a divine element 'falls' into the material realm and lodges itself within certain human beings; from [there] it may be returned to the divine realm through a process of awakening [or revelation] (leading toward salvation)." This is similar to Buddhist meditation unto enlightenment (*bodhi*), or Hindu yoga and tantric practice, which moves one from the world of illusion (*maya*) to terminate the so-called "wheel of karma" that drives reincarnation. "The salvation of the individual thus mirrors a concurrent restoration of the divine nature; a central Gnostic innovation was to elevate individual redemption to the level of a cosmically significant event."[5]

If the teachings of the Gnostics also sound vaguely familiar, they should. Troubling similarities exist between the teachings of Gnosticism and certain glory teachers. Of course, unlike the

Gnostic teachings just described, their teachings are manifestly expressed in Christian language. In fairness, a variety of teachings exist within this movement, and some may stand the test after being sifted. This is a significant issue in the modern church, and it deserves thoughtful attention and proper diligence.

> Thus says the LORD, "Stand by the ways and see and ask for the ancient paths, where the good way is, and walk in it; then you will find a resting place for your souls. But they said, 'We will not walk in it.'"
>
> —JEREMIAH 6:16, NASB

Let us stand in the ancient paths as we consider these two winds of doctrine blowing through the church. Let us neither make the mistake of Jeremiah's contemporaries who refused to receive the admonishment of the Lord nor make the mistake of those who accepted false doctrine and departed from the faith during the early church.

None of this is written to call out any one teacher or group of teachers but rather to establish a framework for thinking about these twin emphases that are at play within the worldwide church. We do so to try to understand what is useful and what should be set aside.

September 1. 2011—
Southern California and Dallas

Recently I co-led a series of public and private meetings in various parts of Southern California with a friend from Australia, Jerry. Most Americans have never heard of Jerry; he's what I would call a "nonconformist" kind of prophet. He calls things like they are, without much concern for how people in church circles feel about it. But I trust him implicitly; and when he prays, things happen.

At these meetings, spiritual phenomena across the spectrum took place. Quite a bit of physical healing occurred, including several people healed of endocrine disorders and one woman healed of neuralgia at a couple's home. Afterward, oil mysteriously appeared on the walls. (This reminded me of a San Francisco-based church known for the phenomenon of oil running down the walls and windows.) Jerry and I led a meeting at a Foursquare Church, where some folks had come up from San Diego. They reported that after the prayer they received, they saw the Lord visit their churches in greater power and with increased healing. The phenomena we saw really seem to be transferable.

In Huntington Beach, many people received empowerment for ministry, and one person's uneven leg grew out. A great deal of skepticism surrounds growing legs because people can easily shift in a chair to create the false impression of growth. But this leg actually grew. There was also a man who was healed of emphysema. Additionally, a teenage girl who requested prayer for nightmares and night terrors afterward reported that all of them had stopped.

After we finished up in Southern California, we headed to Texas. Dallas was hot, but in all the right ways! The Lord's favor definitely went before us. We had thought we would be ministering to a smaller group from a house church, but by the last night we had nearly three hundred people! The ministry was powerful and intense. As has become common, there were several waves of empowerment and deliverance. Among the physical healings: a woman who had arches created in her formerly flat feet! Many in that meeting physically inspected her feet and could testify to the existence of the new arches.

September 9, 2011— Moree, New South Wales, Australia

I am in Australia with Jerry. The first night we were sitting around the campfire on the edge of the outback when Jerry said, "He's out there, about two hundred meters away. I can feel him."

"Who?" I asked.

"The elder," Jerry replied. "He's watching us."

The elder is literally that, the elder of an Aboriginal tribe. He's human, but he carries an unbelievable amount of spiritual power. If he "points the bone" at you (meaning, he literally points the bone at you), unless there's someone around to help you who knows how to counteract that kind of power, you are going to die. Such things are well known in Aboriginal circles.

Jerry and I shared a tent, and that night he awakened with a sense that the elder was standing outside. Jerry spoke to him, saying, "We don't mean any harm."

Sometime later that night, I woke up myself, feeling a disturbance. I opened my eyes to find an off-white-colored hawk inside our tent, even though we had zipped it up completely before we went to sleep.

"You don't belong here," I said. "Leave our tent." Then I rolled over and went back to sleep.

In the morning an off-white feather rested just outside our tent flap where we had put down rubber mats to wipe our feet. Jerry, who got up before I did, picked it up and laid it on his cot, so I didn't know about it until later.

Meanwhile, I got up to walk about. While in the bush, I saw a man about two hundred meters away. He was clearly of Melanesian extraction, dark like weathered rosewood and wearing an off-white cloth about his waist with a sash of the same material that ran from his right shoulder across his chest and stomach to the waistcloth. He appeared to be perhaps seventy or eighty years old; he was standing upright, watching me, holding a spear in his right hand. I pointed at him to let him know I saw him—and just then the white hawk appeared again.

He hovered above me and came closer and closer, so I held out my hand and said, "Come closer, friend. You are welcome to land on my hand. I mean you no harm." The bird hovered very near to me for about two or three minutes, then caught a thermal and flew to a branch in a tree thirty or forty meters away. It landed and watched me.

I looked back to where the man had been standing; he was gone. For some minutes the bird watched me, then flew to another tree, this time farther away. Again it landed and watched me, so again I offered my hand and bade it come to me. It remained perched in the tree, and the man did not reappear, so after some time I turned and walked back to our camp.

When I returned, I shared the story with Jerry. It was then that he handed me the feather. He said, "Did the bird have this color?" Yes, that was it, exactly the color and pattern.

On our way back to Sydney, Jerry and I visited his spiritual father, George. When we described what had happened in the bush, George said, "Yes that was him. I know him, but he hasn't been seen around here for many years." George leads a Foursquare Church and had been part of the Aboriginal mission in the area many years before. He is wise in the ways of the Spirit and of deliverance.

Upon returning to Sydney, I searched for pictures of Australian raptors on the internet. I found a few that looked similar to the bird I had seen, but none that looked the same. It then dawned on me that the elder whom Jerry had sensed, the hawk that had appeared to me in the night, the man I had seen in the bush, and the bird that nearly landed on me were all one and the same.

In the old way of the Aboriginals, changing shapes was well known. These types of behaviors are well documented in Mircea Eliade's outstanding work *Shamanism: Archaic Techniques of Ecstasy.* Eliade was a world-renowned, non-Christian sociologist and anthropologist at the University of Chicago who documented people who could shift shapes or be run through with spears, unharmed, right before his eyes. It was assigned to me as a textbook for a class I took while I was at university in the early 1980s; the fact that someone with academic credibility studied this phenomenon has stayed in my mind for the last forty years.

I gained further insight when, before returning to Moree, I spoke with one of the Aboriginals who had been saved during a move of the Spirit there twenty-five years earlier. He recounted that during that revival, at strange times and places, always unbidden, elders appeared to some of the youth of his people. Their purpose was to warn the youth who were coming to Christ, and many subsequently forsook their professions of faith. When I asked what had become of the spirituality of the Aboriginals during the ensuing years, he said that many of them were "nothing." That is to say, they were neither in touch with Aboriginal spirituality nor did they have a Christian spirituality. They had simply ceased to believe in or practice spirituality at all.

My experience led me to a realization: much modern theology (I am thinking of the writings of men like Bultmann and Tillich and Schweitzer, and even of some "Evangelicals") is so divorced from the worldview of Jesus and the apostles that those teachers and their followers literally are unable to understand New Testament spirituality as it was originally described. To interpret properly the meaning of verses like, "Truly, truly, I say to you,

you will see heaven opened, and the angels of God ascending and descending on the Son of Man" (John 1:51) requires a worldview that has all but vanished from the Western world.

My trip to the outback left me wanting to spend more time among the Aboriginals, ministering the truth of Jesus to them but also learning of their understanding of the spirit world. I hope the opportunity comes again.

September 18, 2011— Melbourne, Australia

The first few days in Melbourne featured visits to churches in Mitcham/Nunawading and the Yarra Valley. Afterward, we went to an Anglican renewal conference hosted at a prominent church in a wealthy suburb. The deliverance anointing continued in these two churches, with one deliverance in particular at Yarra Valley catching my attention.

It started as the "usual stuff," if such a thing can be said. Among the issues from which the Holy Spirit freed people were drug use, sexual immorality or perversion, and dabbling in the occult. All of these things will open the door to demonic oppression. (This is not an exhaustive list, but it gives a sense of the kinds of things that can create open doors in people's lives. Satan will exploit those things to create captivity and bondage.) Oftentimes when people come into Christian faith, particularly from a non-Christian religious background, they may pray the prayer of conversion without actually getting set free from the things that bind them.

However, after driving eight demons from a certain young man, I stopped and asked aloud, "Jesus, is there anything else?" whereupon I received an impression in my mind that was so clear that it was nearly audible: "comic books." I had never considered comic books to be problematic, and I know next to nothing about them. I haven't read one for more than thirty years. However, the man had one come to mind that featured a Japanese heroine. It turned out that a spirit behind that comic book was using the heroine's name. Subsequent ministry led the man to recall several more comic books and deliverance from several more demons associated with their protagonists and titles. You can't make this stuff up! [We wound up driving more than six hundred demons out of him—individually and by name. It took five sessions of roughly two hours each over a period of several visits, but today that man is in the ministry.]

I know for some this will evoke memories of ministers who "see demons behind every tree," but I assure you a) I wasn't "demon hunting"; b) these were real demons; and c) they came out in Jesus' name. At one point, anticipating all the vomit that sometimes accompanies deliverance, we moved outdoors so as not to soil the carpet in the meeting hall. The person for whom I was praying positioned himself over a storm grate, and as I spoke to the various spirits, he spat, spewed, and vomited through the grate into the drain. You could hear it all spattering at the bottom, which was both graphic and glorious at once. Freedom visited that young man that night, with a visible shift in his countenance following the session.

The conference meetings have been powerful and profound. More than fifty churches participated, including twenty Anglican congregations. Several big moves of the Holy Spirit occurred, and in a couple of the sessions, hundreds were touched. One woman was healed of night blindness. We also had what one prophet called a "river of healing" similar to the Pool of Bethesda open up in one localized area of the church sanctuary. One of the prophets said he saw two angels guarding the river—one dressed in a multicolored robe and the other in a silver-white robe with gold trim. Quite a bit of healing happened as people stepped into that river. Later, an engineer who had come with eight friends from his church in Geelong told me he had also seen both angels. So we had two independent witnesses.

[For those who've never been in a meeting where the Spirit of God is moving in a material and tangible way, the language I'm using here could be confusing. But in a time of outpouring, God will often make His presence visible in just this manner. Something similar must have happened in Acts 8:14–24, when Simon the Sorcerer tried to buy the Holy Spirit from the apostle Peter.]

I believe those meetings will accelerate the move of the Spirit across Melbourne and Victoria. Real bridge-building was going on between churches and denominations, and I overheard many accounts of individual pastors making plans to meet and collaborate after the fact.

September 19, 2011— Melbourne

Yesterday the vicar's wife and I led a group of children and young adults in a Holy Spirit encounter service. She asked me to share some stories, which I did. Then we moved to ministry time, and it was like a bomb went off in the room.

We first prayed for a young girl of about twelve with a ruptured spinal disc. (I have no idea how someone that young ruptures a disc, but that's what happened.) When she stood up to receive prayer, the Holy Spirit fell on her and suddenly she jumped, touched her toes, and so on. The other kids went wild, then things really took off. It was crackling!

Tonight after the men's meeting, the vicar and his family joined me in praying for a man's deliverance. We went for about ninety minutes, and I'm glad we had a big bucket! The girls' eyes were like saucers, but when I invited them to cast a couple of demons out, they did it with great authority. Out they came! I jokingly told the vicar that I thought the archdiocese might have its next two candidates for exorcist now ready to apply.

October 6, 2011— Australia

The national gathering of a certain church movement in Australia ended today. I spoke there at their invitation.

For me, the high point was Wednesday night. The worship was absolutely incredible, and at one point, it broke into something that sounded tribal and mysterious. It was unlike anything I had ever been around. Then the voice of prophecy began stirring in the room with several words that hit like a thunderclap. A man I'll call Bruce had a word about the Lord loosing angels, and it almost exactly mirrored the wording of a prayer a few of us had said before the service began.

The last word came forth from Kathy when she read the entire passage from which I was just about to preach! She had no idea it was my passage, and as she was reading it, I said aloud from the other side of the room, "No way! I'm preaching on that exact passage tonight!" Only a few people immediately nearby heard me, but they were visibly surprised too—and shaken. When Kathy finished, someone told her I was planning to speak from that passage, and she too was shaken.

This helped both of us with our faith. It helped Kathy because she had been hesitant to share the Word, and her husband had cajoled her into it. She had wondered if it was from the Lord, if she was grandstanding, if it was weird, or if she had made it up. (You know, the usual things that stop us from prophesying publicly.) When I stood up to preach from that passage, it helped her grow stronger in her discernment of God's voice and in her confidence that God wants to use her prophetically. Meanwhile, I had been battling various struggles, including feeling intimidated and a sense that the anointing just wasn't with me. So her word really emboldened me to just run wide open. I felt an unusual grace in speaking that night.

The ministry time was one of those classic ones that went for over three hours. The Spirit of the Lord visibly broke out all over the room. There was prophetic impartation, calling people into destinies, sovereign infillings, baptisms in the Holy Spirit with shaking and great boldness in utterance, and numerous healings. Many began speaking in tongues. One very notable event occurred when the Holy Spirit fell on a member of our online forum. Several years ago, three of his fingers had been severed by a router as he worked on a piece of wood. Well, they began to regrow! All was captured on the ubiquitous iPhones as the fingers grew out more than one full centimeter over a ninety-minute period. The prayer time for him went far into the night. By this morning, new hair had begun growing on the digits that had grown out, and nail beds were reappearing at the tips. For reasons of His own, the Lord did not complete the healing last night or this morning, but perhaps over the coming days the healing process will be completed. [I contacted the man a few months ago to see what happened, and for whatever reason, the growth had stalled at that point.]

Another high point for me was watching the Holy Spirit fall on a professor from a theological college in Sydney. The level of power was astonishing and terrifying, and she *loved* it! I think hers would be the courses I would want to take if I were attending that seminary. We need more professors of theology to encounter the God who is not a theory.

Tonight I received a message from a woman in Melbourne who'd had a follow-up with her physician. Since the conference, her high blood pressure has fallen into "nearly normal" range, and she is thrilled. So that's a medical confirmation of the work the Lord did among this movement.

The Lord has a way of amazing us, and this trip has been full of surprises. It's fun traveling with Jesus.

November 13, 2011—
Sydney, Australia

I've had a couple of inquiries from people about the prophetic conference that we concluded in Western Sydney yesterday.

The prophetic activations went very well. People were eager to try things out, but at the same time they were afraid. Why? Well, first and foremost, they were afraid they would be wrong or that the words they shared might be inaccurate. Some were afraid they wouldn't get any prophetic words from God. However, the Lord was very generous in releasing people into highly accurate levels of prophetic anointing. One exercise was structured so that each person received five separate words from five separate people who were physically separated, and consequently none of the five prophesiers could possibly know the words the other prophesiers had given or that each person had already been receiving. In each case, people had the same word confirmed over and over as they went from one prophesier to another. Now *that* raised people's faith. It also helped the ones who were prophesying to know that they themselves weren't making it up. All in all, I was very pleased with the outcome of that exercise.

December 5, 2011—
Dallas

I feel the need to write something preemptively about the feathers that are appearing in Spirit-filled meetings in Texas. This is because someone asked me what I think about theology versus experience, suggesting that perhaps this was too "experience-oriented" rather than "theology-oriented."

The short answer is that I favor *both*. I believe in robust, sound theology, and I try to incorporate it into my messages. On the other hand, I don't think Orthodox theology should be sterile and dry. Saint Anselm wrote of *fides quaerens intellectum*, or "faith seeking understanding." Saint Anselm was one of the greatest theological thinkers of the Late Dark Ages (which were not dark at all), and he was also a great worker of miracles with a very accurate prophetic gift. The Westminster catechism says we are to serve God and to *enjoy* Him forever. You can't enjoy what you do not experience. So theology should help us interpret our experiences, but our experiences should complement our theology and give it life.

Now back to the feathers. I really have no idea what they mean. They have appeared in a few meetings I've led but not all. I don't seek them, and I don't preach about them in my messages. In other meetings where they have fallen, people have tried to explain them, but I don't think anyone *really* knows what they mean. However, the Lord has seemed pleased in this season to release them over some meetings from time to time. These are His meetings, after all, dedicated to Him. If He wants to release feathers, so be it. Who are we to question Him for doing so? I will be the first to admit that no part of Scripture describes feathers appearing as part of a normal worship service. But since there isn't really anything about feathers appearing that *contradicts* Scripture, I don't see a deep theological problem with them. The concern would come if people begin rushing from place to place hoping to see feathers, then collecting them, venerating them, and ultimately worshiping them. However, if we simply keep them in their proper context as a sign of God's presence among us and of His imagination, creativity, and love—just one sign of many that He has given and might choose to give in the future—we will remain grounded in the Word.

PILLAR 2

Purity

Speak to all the congregation of the people
of Israel and say to them, You shall be holy,
for I the LORD your God am holy.
—LEVITICUS 19:2

You shall be holy to me, for I the LORD am holy and have
separated you from the peoples, that you should be mine.
—LEVITICUS 20:26

For you are a people holy to the LORD your
God, and the LORD has chosen you to be a
people for his treasured possession, out of all the
peoples who are on the face of the earth.
—DEUTERONOMY 14:2

As obedient children, do not be conformed to the
passions of your former ignorance, but as he who called
you is holy, you also be holy in all your conduct, since
it is written, "You shall be holy, for I am holy."
—1 PETER 1:14–16

FOR MANY EVANGELICALS and River Stream/Fourth Wave Charismatics, the word *holiness* conjures up stale images of revival meetings, gospel trios, and old-time religion—along with stern prohibitions against drinking, dancing, cussing, and playing cards. Despite a declining number of people who grew up in such settings, the images persist, and many are happy to leave these notions of holiness in the past. Yet while it seems we've cast off the old, legalistic dogmas regarding holiness, often we've merely replaced them. In our era of techno-savvy megachurches and postmodern emerging churches, holiness (when it is discussed at all) is commonly reduced to moral behavior: sexual purity, financial honesty, no drinking, no drugs, commitment to private Bible study and prayer, and so on. When this occurs, it is all too easy for believers to relegate holiness to a small, albeit hopefully important, part of our private lives. This scenario, though common, is far from biblical.

Religion has become internal and subjective rather than external and objective. This is, in part, behind the rise of the new mysticism; in a world where we divorce our practice of religion from external benchmarks and specific behaviors, all that remains is internal visions, hearing voices, and supernatural transportation. It's not that these things are wrong; it is that they are not enough for a robust Christian spirituality, which should include accountability to one another for Christlike character. Additionally, internal and subjective religion will never change a culture.

Said another way, we have favored personal standards over biblical standards of holiness in our quest for "cultural relevance." This is defended in the name of winning others to Christ. "If we talk about holiness with unbelievers," so the argument goes, "won't that just present another hurdle for them to overcome on their way to Christ?" For this and other reasons, we are rapidly forsaking our historic commitment to the pursuit of biblical holiness. Recent polls indicate that many self-described Evangelicals and Charismatics march in moral lockstep with mainstream Western culture in practices of divorce, spousal abuse, extramarital sex, pornography consumption, materialism, self-importance (pride), and racism, to name just a few. To this list, we can also add that we have essentially conceded on the matter of homosexuality.

While we are busy tipping our hats to the importance of cultural relevance, however, our culture no longer views us as different in any meaningful way, except for those who see us as hypocrites failing to live what we supposedly believe. That is a shame.

I believe this overall situation has a single underlying cause: as with so many biblical concepts, "holiness" is no longer understood to mean what it originally meant in biblical thought. To be sure, the biblical terms translated "holy" or "holiness" (*qadosh* in Hebrew and *hagios* in Greek) carry a strong connotation of moral purity. But moral purity is not, primarily, the essence of biblical holiness, though it does carry great importance. I'll say that again: Moral purity is not, primarily, the essence of holiness. Rather, to be holy is to be set apart.

Holiness, as it pertains to God, is the quality by which God is set apart unto Himself. He is utterly unlike any other thing or person or being or experience in the universe. The beauty of His holiness is that He is so unique and incomparable. We may say that He is "like" this or that, but the truth is that He is really "*un*like" this or that. He may be love, but He is unlike flawed human love. He may be our Father, but He is unlike our fallen earthly fathers. He has no beginning, yet even the universe had a beginning. He has no end, yet all other things we have ever known will come to an end. He cannot be corrupted, yet all we have ever known is eminently corruptible humanity. I could go on, but you get the idea.

Holiness, as it pertains to humans, speaks to the fact that we are called to be "set apart" or "dedicated" to God. "I will be your God, and you will be my people," says Yahweh. (See Leviticus 26:12 and Hebrews 8:10.) We belong to God. We are not to be like the nations around us. We are to live differently. Consider the following passages of Scripture:

> When the LORD your God brings you into the land that
> you are entering to take possession of it, and clears away

many nations before you, the Hittites, the Girgashites, the Amorites, the Canaanites, the Perizzites, the Hivites, and the Jebusites, seven nations more numerous and mightier than you, and when the LORD your God gives them over to you, and you defeat them, then you must devote them to complete destruction. You shall make no covenant with them and show no mercy to them. You shall not intermarry with them, giving your daughters to their sons or taking their daughters for your sons, for they would turn away your sons from following me, to serve other gods. Then the anger of the LORD would be kindled against you, and he would destroy you quickly. But thus shall you deal with them: you shall break down their altars and dash in pieces their pillars and chop down their Asherim and burn their carved images with fire. For you are a people holy to the LORD your God. The LORD your God has chosen you to be a people for his treasured possession, out of all the peoples who are on the face of the earth.

—DEUTERONOMY 7:1–6

When the LORD your God cuts off before you the nations whom you go in to dispossess, and you dispossess them and dwell in their land, take care that you be not ensnared to follow them, after they have been destroyed before you, and that you do not inquire about their gods, saying, "How did these nations serve their gods?—that I also may do the same." You shall not worship the LORD your God in that way, for every abominable thing that the LORD hates they have done for their gods, for they even burn their sons and their daughters in the fire to their gods.

—DEUTERONOMY 12:29–31

When you come into the land that the LORD your God is giving you, you shall not learn to follow the abominable practices of those nations. There shall not be found among you anyone who burns his son or his daughter as an offering, anyone who practices divination or tells fortunes or interprets omens, or a sorcerer or a charmer or a medium or a

necromancer or one who inquires of the dead, for who-
ever does these things is an abomination to the LORD.
And because of these abominations the LORD your God is
driving them out before you. You shall be blameless before
the LORD your God, for these nations, which you are about
to dispossess, listen to fortune-tellers and to diviners. But as
for you, the LORD your God has not allowed you to do this.

—DEUTERONOMY 18:9–14

Hear the word that the LORD speaks to you, O house of
Israel. Thus says the LORD: "Learn not the way of the
nations, nor be dismayed at the signs of the heavens because
the nations are dismayed at them, for the customs of the
peoples are vanity."

—JEREMIAH 10:1–3

What is in your mind shall never happen—the thought,
"Let us be like the nations, like the tribes of the countries,
and worship wood and stone."

—EZEKIEL 20:32

Here is what these five passages have in common: a clear
calling for God's people to be set apart unto Him. Prior to any
consideration of morality, biblical holiness describes a unique relationship that God desires to have with His people. Because this
covenant relationship is unique among all other relationships that
He has with His creation, and because God Himself (not humans)
has established it, He has the right to ask, require, yes, even to
demand certain standards of behavior from His people (i.e., from
us) because He can, because He is God. We don't attain righteousness in following these commandments, but neither can we
legitimately say that we are His if we do not follow them.

Holiness begins with a relationship with God, but it also has
definite moral ramifications. These may require—even in the
New Testament era—that we *not* live or look like the people in our
surrounding culture. The quotation from 1 Peter 1:14–16, written

to New Testament believers, makes this clear. Furthermore, Christian behaviors and practices should flow from the fact that Christians are "a chosen race, a royal priesthood, a holy nation, a people for [God's] own possession, that [we] may proclaim the excellencies of him who called [us] out of darkness into his marvelous light" (1 Pet. 2:9).

So what kinds of behaviors are forbidden to Christians? Well, looking at the five passages of Scripture just quoted, we see idolatry (or the worship of other gods alongside of God, on any level); adopting the "customs" of the people around us (which includes a wide range of behaviors variously listed throughout the Scriptures, omitted here for the sake of brevity and irenic discourse); intermarrying (because of the risk of syncretism, the blending of two or more religious systems; this is why Paul prohibits Christians from marrying nonbelievers in 2 Corinthians 6:14); killing (or aborting) our children; and engaging in the black arts, a subset of a wider class of New Age and pagan religious practices. This is not an exhaustive list, but it does represent some of the behaviors that commonly ensnare Christians. Perhaps reading this will stir thoughts of others.

This can be profoundly confusing; in the modern context, many Christians have been told to be as much like the people around them as possible in order to "win the lost." The meager harvest tells a different story. While Christians should be approachable and affable, holiness may ultimately be more attractive than assimilation. After all, if Christians act like nonbelievers, what is the point of becoming a Christian?

A look at biblical holiness through the lens of Jesus as the unique revelation of God brings the common emphasis on morals into a more proper balance. Think of it: those who have responded in faith to the revelation of God in Jesus Christ have been united with Him through the Holy Spirit. In other words, in Christ we are already holy because we have been joined to God's holiness.

Before we are ever called to be good or to refrain from any specific behaviors, we are called to be found in Him. "Goodness" flows from holiness, not the other way around.

Said another way, Christianity is a living, organic relationship; God Himself, in the person of the indwelling Holy Spirit, motivates everything. In Christ we participate in the very life and holiness of God. Unless we rightly understand and affirm the primacy of this relationship, we fall into the inevitable trap of reducing holiness to mere morality and legalism. With these thoughts in mind, however, we begin to see how much more God is asking of us. As long as our notions of holiness are limited to doing certain things and not doing other things, we can go through our entire lives obeying the rules (or at least maintaining the appearance of doing so) without dealing with the more fundamental questions: To whom do we belong? To whom do we give our first love and loyalty? Are we prepared to make our lives like He would have them look, irrespective of our own customs, habits, and preferences?

In the end God's call to be holy is an all-encompassing claim on our lives, our loves, and our identities. It is a reaffirmation of discipleship that may require us to stop doing certain things that we like to do, to refrain from doing certain things we have considered, or to start doing things that we would rather not do. It means that everything a Christian is and has belongs to God, and every aspect of life is to be shaped and directed toward God. To be a disciple of Jesus Christ requires nothing less than death to our fallen self-focus in order to live in and for Him.

> For whoever would save his life will lose it, but whoever loses his life for my sake and the gospel's will save it. For what does it profit a man to gain the whole world and forfeit his soul?
>
> —Mark 8:35–36

To sum up, holiness is primarily about union with God in Christ and sharing in Christ's holiness. It is secondarily about living life as God requires. Out of these two, service to God and to others will naturally and abundantly flow. Only a biblical, Christ-centered holiness will safeguard Evangelicals and Charismatics from the twin traps of legalistic moralism and lawlessness. This is how the church can recover its spiritual footing in today's world and win the lost. As I travel in a culture that is very different from my own, I am struck by how pressing and relevant these matters are to Christians here, who live as a distinct minority with beliefs and customs that are decidedly different from their neighbors. The same "separateness" should be the experience of *every* Christian, whether American or Australian, English or Canadian, German or Israeli, Chinese or Sri Lankan, Mexican or Costa Rican. Holiness is a summons that God issues to all Christians everywhere, and it will be a hallmark of the coming visitation.

"Be holy [different], for I am holy [different]," says the Lord (1 Pet. 1:16, MEV).

January 23, 2012—
A Major Middle Eastern Capital City

If anyone thinks that Muslims can't/won't/don't get saved, they should come to the Middle East to watch them respond to words of knowledge and prophecy. If that's not enough, they should watch what happens when curses placed on them by their in-laws or neighbors are broken and their demons come out. Jesus loves Muslims, and it looks like He is about to start bringing a *lot* of them into the kingdom. I am hearing reports of what is happening in various cities out here, and something is definitely afoot.

The last two meetings here in the Middle East have gone past 2:30 a.m. The people are that hungry. Wow! The patience and perseverance are incredible. One woman waited for prayer four-and-a-half hours last night, then another three hours tonight. When I finally got to her, she showed me pictures of her family on her phone, and I began getting prophetic words for them. One man tonight waited five hours for prayer.

Several people have received prayer for their involvement in magic, palmistry, fortune-telling, and more. I was intrigued to learn that one young woman and her brother, after receiving prayer last night, went home and somewhat hastily "spilled the beans" to their mother, who was very unhappy about what was happening. However, when the mother came to the meeting tonight, she gave her life to Christ! I am more convinced than ever that signs and wonders are important keys to unlocking the Middle East for the Lord; on this trip alone, I've led well over three hundred people to Him. I can't wait to come back here! I love it.

March 5, 2012—
Jayapura, Papua, Indonesia

Yesterday we had two meetings. During the morning service, there was a release of the Spirit on the elders and leaders of the church. Afterward, we asked them to pray for the congregation, and immediately a massive move of the Spirit occurred; almost every person was hit by the power of God (which they experienced from the floor because they couldn't stand up). Most of them hadn't encountered something like this in a long time, if ever. The Spirit seemed to be reminding everyone that leadership means service. The meeting that night was outstanding. Simply put, open hearts move with the Spirit.

Last night's youth meeting was really something to behold. To begin with, the room we occupied didn't have the ventilation of the main church building, and I don't think I'm exaggerating to say that the temperature was north of 120 degrees Fahrenheit (roughly 49 degrees Celsius). When we were finished, we were soaked. Anyway, we had a few hundred youths gather, and they sat on the floor. These young adults were *hungry* and kept interrupting my message with applause, shouts of *amin* (which is "amen" in most of the rest of the world outside the former British Commonwealth) and "Yes, Lord!" (in Bahasa and their native languages). When I finished preaching, I called the team up, and we began to deliver prophetic words over the crowd. Some were overcome by the power of God as the prophecies hit them. This sent the faith level soaring. God was there! Then it happened: a massive move of the Spirit broke out before we were even done delivering the words we had to give. Many never got up off the floor. Instead, they simply fell over where they sat. For more than eighty minutes, the Spirit moved as the youth received from the Lord. It sounded like the Day of Pentecost. The noise was *so* loud that Jerry had to have the PA turned up as he tried to give his message in the next building. The sound of those being filled with the Spirit was drowning out his amplified voice!

Then we began to pray for those who had prophetic or evangelistic callings, and pastoral/teaching callings, each group by turn. Those who responded to these altar calls were cut down as with a scythe and lay in piles on the floor, some for nearly two hours. Bodies lay everywhere, many stacked across and on top of each other. Healings broke out everywhere, as did deliverances.

One of the most interesting deliverances was of a young woman who had not one but two shaman spirits as well as a spirit of fear. Her father, an elder who was getting set free in Jerry's meeting the next building over, had been a shaman, and that generational inheritance was decisively broken. Such is the power of the cross to defeat Satan and his schemes.

Finally, we prayed for everyone left who hadn't been in any of the prophetic/evangelistic/pastor-teacher groups. We never really got to most of them as they were falling like dominoes, many simply dropping unconscious. Maria Woodworth-Etter had meetings in the 1880s in which she described "the battlefields of the Lord" and the innumerable "slain of the Lord." This was that.

When we all finally left the meeting, we were drained and in shock. This church will never be the same, and I expect that will be true of Jayapura as well. We have an open healing meeting today, and we have encouraged everyone to bring every sick person they know in the entire city. I expect to see many, many healings, miracles, and salvations before we leave tomorrow for a small village in the mountains.

"So there was much rejoicing in that city" (Acts 8:8, NASB).

March 6, 2012—
Wamena, Papua

This morning we flew into this valley surrounded by high mountains that run like a spine across the whole of Papua (Indonesia) and Papua New Guinea (formerly Britain-Australia, but now independent). For those who have studied missions or the political history of Oceania and the South Pacific, Papua was once known as Irian Jaya, and in this town some markers still bear that name.

After arriving, we went to our hotel to freshen up for lunch. The team then traveled some distance out of town into the foothills of the mountains. There, we found an entire village of Papuans living in grass huts. The men all wore the *koteka* (a covering for the private parts made from a dried gourd), and the women wore only grass skirts. Seeing this village gave new meaning to Genesis 2:25, which mentions Adam and Eve being naked and unashamed, and I can assure all readers that there was nothing erotic or even suggestive about how these people carried themselves; quite the contrary, in fact. A few of the people wore scant items of Western garb, including one man who had a New York Yankees ball cap on. Go figure.

The villagers brought a mummy of one of their ancestors to show us. He is kept in the chief's hut and was killed by the Dutch about three hundred sixty years ago in a battle that has long since been forgotten by all but these villagers, at a location that probably will never be known. The mummy was completely black, and he was sitting as these people do, on his haunches. He still wore a *koteka*, long since broken about halfway down. We were told that other mummies were in the village, but we did not see them. We started by praying with the chief. He was immediately healed of a spinal issue that had him bent double in pain, then the entire village surged forward seeking prayer. All but one of the roughly twenty we prayed for reported being completely healed of all sorts of ailments—skin diseases, blindness, deafness, digestive issues, and so on—within two minutes.

A team of Hungarian anthropologists was there studying this tribe, and they spoke excellent English. They caught the entire healing service on film and told us it will be broadcast on Hungarian television in the future.

This evening's service at the church was lengthy, with essentially three sermons. The ministry time was quiet, with many falling down under the power of the Spirit; but not all did so. We had assumed that God would surely visit them with great power after the receptivity we saw in the village earlier that day. It was completely different, however, from what we had experienced in Jayapura—very difficult to get started, very difficult for the people to receive, and certainly not explosive.

Partway through the ministry time, several of us noticed that we each had prayed for multiple women with stumps for fingers. We all got our translators to ask the women why they were missing fingers. It turns out that in Baliem culture, the women (but not the men) cut off a finger each time a family member dies! Then we understood that even though this practice had been stopped recently, the abuse, grief, binding to death, the soul/spirit ties to departed loved ones/ancestors (Remember the mummy in the village?), and the misogyny that is embedded in the culture has been hindering the work of the Spirit.

Tomorrow we intend to address this cluster of issues, and based on past sessions of this type, both Jerry and I expect things to get very, very messy as the demonic strongholds that have bound these people for centuries get broken. Although the people in the church are Christian, most have never had deliverance, including from the ancestral bondage that comes from cutting oneself for the dead (Lev. 19:28). God knew what He was talking about when He banned these kinds of practices in the Old Testament.

March 7, 2012—
Wamena

In the morning service I spoke on the culture of death, the spirit of death, and the law of the spirit of life in Christ Jesus. I used several texts for my message, including Hebrews 2:14–16, Leviticus 19:28, Romans 8:2, and 1 Corinthians 15:55. Notwithstanding, even with *two* translators (one for Indonesian, the other for Baliem), the entire message took less than thirty-two minutes. That means that my piece (in English) was less than eleven minutes long. (Please spread the word to those who still think I can't preach short messages!)

The ministry time, however, was not short. We finally broke around 12:30 p.m. after praying about the spirit and culture of death, breaking ancestral worship over the crowd, and then taking an extended time to receive the numerous testimonies from people who had been touched either last night or this morning.

One woman, who was related to the mummy I mentioned yesterday, was delivered of an ancestral spirit (as if anyone was surprised). Her friend, the daughter of a local chief, was delivered of a spirit that had regional control over part of this valley. Jerry and I prayed for this one together, but I stepped back at one point and took a picture of him standing over the woman as she foamed at the mouth. He was pointing at the door, saying in English, "Get out! Leave the area! You aren't wanted here anymore!" The woman retched, rolled over, shuddered, and it was over. She gave a tremendous testimony, whereupon the Holy Spirit fell on her, and she ended up back on the floor. Several members of the team prophesied that she has a ministry of bringing the gospel to her people. She then told us that her husband had died recently, and all she wanted was to bring a power-filled gospel back to her people. *Ka-ching!*

Tonight's meeting featured Jerry preaching on the Father's love.

Though simple, it was one of the more profound messages I have heard. Jerry used a stick to illustrate two faces of a father: the harsh one who beats people and the loving one who hugs them and helps them out of their misery. He then talked about husbands who are like barking dogs, growling and snarling at their wives and children, and about wives who are like clucking hens, pecking at their husbands. A time of reconciliation between husbands and wives followed, and there wasn't a dry eye in the room.

Then the children were brought in, and more tears flowed. The healing service afterward saw a person healed of blindness, a cataract vanish, and a woman with emphysema able to breathe deeply and freely once again (presumably healed, although in this remote environment we didn't have the medical capability to confirm it).

The influence of spirits here is taken for granted. Even for me, it is a tough transition from the rational skepticism of the West. One of the women my translator and I prayed for tonight had severe scoliosis. It came to her two years ago when she went to wash clothes in a river that was a sacred spot. The next morning she woke up to a deformed spine, severe pain, and no strength in her legs. She subsequently went to a witch doctor to seek healing. (Yes she was a Christian, and no, she shouldn't have sought help from the witch doctor. However, when the church has no power, people will go wherever they think they need to in order to find relief. Church, are you listening?) When we began to pray, the spirit would not leave, and at that point I asked whether she had sought help from a witch doctor. When we broke his spell over her, we were then able to drive the spirit out. I have run into a few of these water spirits in the past, and they are cunning. This one was named "Pinte."

[Water spirits hang around bodies of water—rivers, ponds, lakes, wells. Some people make a big deal out of them. I know they're real. They don't generally inhabit human beings, though they will attack them. Spirits' names correspond to their behavior, and occasionally it can be helpful to get their names if we run into difficulty driving them out. But the name might be something you don't expect at all. There are times in deliverance when we must secure the name of the spirit from the spirit itself. This differs in two ways from some prevailing ideology—one belief being that you never have to know a spirit's name, and the other being that you can simply say things like, "All water spirits, leave now!" and still be effective. Those beliefs are not universally true. Jesus had to ask Legion's name, and sometimes so do we. Sometimes we might be able to get people free by calling the spirit out by its activity; other times we might need its actual name. But simply declaring, "I command all evil spirits here to leave in Jesus' name!" and clapping your hands is not effective, in my experience; I have to call them out by name more than half the time. Usually I get the spirit's name myself by word of knowledge, but other times I have to ask.]

March 14, 2012— Serui, Papua

The church here is rather large, and people have put chairs outside around the building to listen to the services. Although there are certainly more people attending the meetings than we could accommodate inside, it is also partly a heat-management solution, as it tends to be a bit cooler outside versus inside. So all the doors and windows are opened, and anyone outside can easily hear.

As in all the local areas we have visited, the church is "embedded" in a neighborhood. Most people simply walk down lanes and paths to get to services. There is no parking lot other than in the children's play area, where you might be able to park a small handful of vehicles at most. The nearest homes are literally two steps from the exterior walls of the church, though not all of these neighbors attend the services. On the other hand, they don't need to attend because there is simply no way they can avoid hearing the music, testimonies, preaching, and so on. More importantly, none of this seems to faze anybody. Talk about cultural contrast! When I think of all the zoning issues, noise ordinances, conditional-use permits, and more, that churches in Australia, Europe, and the United States must deal with, it's almost comical to see this state of affairs.

This morning's meeting at church was one of the more powerful ones we have had. Toward the end, Jerry was outside speaking with a man who had come to his meetings last year in Sorong while I finished inside. It was about noon, and just then the *muezzin* from the mosque next door started his call to prayer. (The same noise dynamics I described for the church also apply to the mosque.) So with the call to prayer resounding in my ears, I walked up to one of the elders to pray. He'd had a stroke in March 2007, although I didn't know that. What I did know was that this man was barely able to shuffle. My translator and I prayed for him a couple of times, then we asked him to try walking. He was able to do so with significantly more mobility; all the pain in his legs and hips had disappeared. We walked him around inside the church while continuing to pray for him. The church erupted into clapping and rejoicing, as the people knew this local elder very well.

Meanwhile, the man from Sorong asked Jerry for prayer so he also could heal the sick, so Jerry laid hands on him and prayed for God to begin using him in healing. Then he told the man to go look for a sick person for whom he could pray. He walked up to a young man who was part of the outside crowd and asked if he needed healing for anything. It turned out that this youth had malaria, and when the man from Sorong laid his hands on him, all the symptoms immediately left. (Note that I say the *symptoms* left him; it would clearly be impossible to verify that the bacteria in his blood were gone without a blood test.) Everyone was astounded and began celebrating.

Just then, another man who had come with the man from Sorong tapped Jerry on the shoulder and said, through the translator, "I don't understand this Jesus. What does it mean?" Whereupon the man from Sorong who had just prayed for the youth with malaria led his friend over to a chair and explained Jesus to him and prayed with him to receive the Lord. Then he laid hands on him to receive the Holy Spirit. Jerry and I had gone into the adjoining building to have lunch, and as we were sitting down, the man from Sorong came in to say that his friend had gotten saved and received the "fire." We went outside to see his friend lying on the pavement, unconscious in the Spirit. All of these things happened before the *muezzin* had finished his call to prayer. There were also about twenty salvations.

This is a small town. To say it is "nestled" in a valley would be too comfortable of a word. It is shoehorned into a valley that backs up against the mountains and then runs down to the sea. The valley is at most a kilometer across. We have put out the word that anyone in town who is sick should come for healing tomorrow night. I expect that we will have a major breakout of healing tomorrow.

March 15, 2012—
Serui

Today was our last day here. It began with a couple of the team fishing from oceangoing dugouts, each equipped with dual outriggers and an outboard motor. The rest of the team and I took one of the two roads out of town and headed east along the coast. This island is too mountainous to accommodate roads that would cross over the top and down to the other side. So instead there is one "loop road" that encircles the island. Driving all the way around it takes more than a day, at least in part because as you get out of town, the pavement begins to break up and becomes filled with potholes and eventually downgrades to a dirt road.

The mountains tumble straight down to the sea, so even with a coastal route, this road can be very windy and steep. It is never more than 1.5 car-widths wide, and there is no center line. Consequently, at virtually every blind turn, our driver must honk the horn to warn oncoming traffic. Oncoming traffic does the same. Of course, with the thick jungle everywhere, visibility is additionally limited by the tropical hardwoods towering hundreds of meters into the sky, the overhanging vines, and the tall grass alongside the road. Virtually every hairpin turn traverses a flow of icy water rushing from the summits to the sea. Although this feels more like Jurassic Park than anywhere I have ever been, modern road signs pop up along the way saying that if you miss your turn, you will end up in the drink. The signs aren't necessary. This is a road that sobers you up quickly.

We traveled east of town for about forty-five minutes until we came to a small village of no more than a dozen homes—typical Indonesian homes, mostly painted in a distinct green, blue, peach, or white. Some were unpainted, no doubt reflecting either the reduced economic state of the owners or perhaps a lack of care. Their roofs were of thatch or corrugated metal; metal is more common, but the thatch is cooler. However, metal does not attract bugs or snakes, which are numerous and frequently poisonous.

In this village, a church had recently been planted. The congregation was expecting us; we were to bless their new building. About fifty people gathered, and a man named Daniel shared a few words. He then invited me and a man named Nick to speak. I began with a few words about the birthing of churches, but the spirit of prophecy was already moving, so I began calling people out of the group and the Spirit started falling. Nick joined in this effort, while our translator rendered everything into Indonesian.

Periodically, people would exclaim, "That's right!" or "God sees!" or "God has visited us!" We didn't prophesy over the entire group, but the accuracy of the words was uncanny. It seemed that the Lord wanted to establish this congregation as a house of prophecy, and we told them so. We left that church with great difficulty as the people thronged us and presented us with papayas larger than American footballs, bunches of fresh bananas, and fresh-cut jungle pineapple. We then drove west back through town, then out the other side on the same coast road.

We stopped at three churches. The first was under construction, with only block walls but no doors or windows yet. Nevertheless, when we walked in, we sensed a healing presence. One particular spot in the church seemed especially anointed for healing, so we asked if anyone from the small congregation who had met us was sick. Two adolescent girls were brought to us. One was an epileptic, and the other had malaria. We stood beside them in the spot that seemed to have the healing anointing, and the power of God fell on both of them, knocking them to the floor. When they stood up, both testified that they felt something leave their bodies as we prayed. I can't say they were healed with only this evidence, but I can say that both girls testified that they had been touched by God and thought they were healed. I am sure we will hear more about them down the road. [We did later find out that both had been healed.]

This church was clearly going to be a house of healing, and the pastor asked us to lay hands on him to heal the sick. He was powerfully touched by the Spirit and fell to the ground on the exact spot where we had sensed the anointing. We told the pastor to look for a sign (John 20:30–31) that the Lord would make his church a house of healing. He asked what that sign would be, and we told him there would be a miraculous catch of large fish. The sea was only thirty meters from the front door of the church building. [We later received word that the men of the church had gone out fishing and hauled in more than two hundred fish in one net. A typical catch for them would have been ten to twenty fish.]

The next church was a smallish building that was nearly complete. As we prayed, we felt led to break a heaviness that was resting over it. A large black wasp was flying around inside, and we prayed that the sting of death would be broken over that place. We also laid hands on the table where they celebrate communion and asked the Lord to establish a house of miracles in that little clearing where this church stood. While nobody received prophecies or healings, there was something unmistakably good that seemed to enter the room. As we left, I looked back inside and the wasp had vanished. Was this coincidence or a sign? [I'll leave that for you, the reader, to decide.]

We drove to the last church, and on the way I sensed the Holy Spirit saying to me that this congregation would not have to fear mosquitoes. Malaria remains a serious health risk in this area, and mosquitoes are not merely an irritation but a life-threatening pestilence. Fires are sometimes set to create smoke to keep mosquitoes away, similar to citronella coils in Australia and the United States. When we pulled up, the site was nothing more than a bare foundation set in the midst of a lowland swamp. A single lonely mango tree marked the front of the property where it touched the road.

We walked from our vehicles, followed by a few members of the congregation, the pastor, and his wife. Nick and I walked the perimeter of the foundation, then we moved to the inside of the building and stopped right in the center, about two-thirds of the way to the front. As we stood there, I sensed a word forming about the fire of God. [Remember the smoke-mosquito-protection I previously mentioned.] But before I could say anything, Nick suddenly exclaimed, "I see a pillar of fire at each corner of this building! The Lord is establishing a house of fire!" At that, I turned to the pastor's wife, laid my hand on her head, and said, "The Lord has seen your faithfulness. Receive the fire and become its carrier." She fell under the power of God, and we carried her to a spot that didn't have weeds and sticks so she could lie under the power in a relatively comfortable area. The pastor's eyes were as large as proverbial saucers. Ho-hum! Just another morning's work in Papua.

Tonight's healing meeting was something to see. About two hundred fifty people were seated inside the church building, with at least that many seated outside. The worship was deeply moving, even for someone who does not speak Indonesian. The young women of the church danced before the congregation with devotion and skill. Then Daniel preached on healing, followed by Jerry, who preached further on healing. At the end of his message, Jerry asked if any deaf people were in the crowd. Ten people came forward, then he asked for the youth who wished to heal the sick to come forward. He specifically asked for youth who had never prayed for anyone to be healed. Ten came forward, all under the age of twenty. Ten out of ten deaf people testified afterward that they had been healed when they received prayer from these young adults. The tenth was a woman who testified that she had lost her hearing fifty-four years ago! Now this got everyone's attention! Jerry then asked the church what they had been doing for fifty-four years, letting this woman suffer with deafness most of her life. He has a unique way with these people that allows him to ask questions like this, whereas most of us would demur rather than risk offending people by being too direct.

Next, Jerry asked anyone who had anything wrong with them at all to stand. He then asked members of the congregation to gather around those needing prayer. I led the ministry outside, while Jerry led the ministry inside the building. I don't know who took the left side, but I do know that *every* person on the right side of the church where I stood was 100 percent healed upon receiving prayer from their fellow church members. Inside, the percentage appeared to be 100 percent as well.

One woman had several breast tumors that had broken through the skin. They simply fell off; she was holding them in her hand as if a bag of what looked like toasted corn had been emptied into her palm. There was also a man who had been paralyzed by a stroke seven years earlier but was walking when we left him tonight. Three of us, along with the youth who led the prayer, worked with him for about an hour. The young people were beside themselves as they watched sensation return to his arm, hand, leg, and foot, then watched him stand and eventually walk. Another woman, also a stroke victim who had been carried into the meeting in a chair, received significant healing, although she was not fully healed. She did recover sensation in her hand, arm, leg, and foot, along with the ability to stand and about half of her grip strength. For the record, this ministry time was essentially led by local "first-timers" who should be able to continue, even after we leave tomorrow. Jerry, Daniel, the team, and I simply orchestrated various parts of this visitation of Jesus.

I know this may stretch some of you, but based on what we have seen here in Indonesia and elsewhere, 100 percent healing seems to be within grasp. When we don't see it, the issue does not seem to be on God's end, but ours. I am pondering this question: "Will we reach out for it?" Another question has to do with the fact that at least a third of the people in the meeting tonight were unsaved. We often find that these people must be led to saving faith (with power, not mere words) before they can be fully healed. This is one (though not the only) secret to healing. However, some are healed before they receive Christ. It is a mystery why God will heal some people before they are saved, while others must confess Jesus first. This is part of His sovereignty in healing.

March 29, 2012—
Adelaide, South Australia

Some noteworthy things took place at our meetings here: A man who was both mute and amnesiac was healed completely, as was a woman with vertigo. This allowed her to resume normal living, including driving. Also, a couple of other people received healing for skeletal conditions, such as extreme knee pain. Both had received prophetic words in coffee shops and grocery stores before the conference, stating that they were about to be healed. How cool is that?

On Sunday afternoon, a wheelchair-bound woman received ministry and the power of the Holy Spirit came on her. I pulled her up, but when she tired, she sat down again. Two days later, we received a text message stating that one of her legs was now healed and the other was half-healed. The next day we received a text stating that both legs were healed and this woman had walked into a Bible study. The pastor of the church and I discussed this healing while driving to Whyalla today, and while we both want to know more about what she is and is not capable of doing, the information we have appears to be credible and verified.

While I was in Indonesia, three stroke victims were healed of paralysis. One of them was partially healed when we left the building that night, so it could have stopped there or the healing could have continued. We don't know the current status on that one, but it was clear that she was significantly improved after three of us prayed for her. However, the other two paralytics were healed and went home walking. So between the three healings in Indonesia and this very recent healing in South Australia, it appears the Lord is opening the doors for healing of paralysis, paraplegia, and quadriplegia. This is something we have seen in years gone by, but not in this quantity or with this rapidity. May the Lord continue to increase this grace upon the church! [At the time of this writing, I have seen well over four hundred paralytics healed.]

April 10, 2012—
Los Angeles

I took a trip to Washington, DC, last week. I had just gotten home from Australia, and frankly I wondered if the many remarkable things that had been happening there and in Indonesia would carry over to the United States, but the Lord settled those concerns. Two people with various degrees of blindness and a woman with rheumatoid arthritis were healed. A broken foot was healed. Also, there was a woman with two titanium rods in her neck and back, and when the Lord was finished with her, she could move her head and neck, whereas before they had been totally immobilized! I found this healing of particular interest because I had once heard someone say that when metal dissolves in the body, a distinctive noxious odor results. When a foul smell arose as we were praying, I knew we were onto something. That woman went home a *very* happy camper and also somewhat dumbfounded as she was now able to move her head and neck in a way that had been impossible before.

There was also a pastor with a chronic wasting condition who was healed. I received an email from him yesterday stating that all his symptoms are gone and he feels better than he has since the disease began. He intends to update us after he gets the results back from the doctor.

The Lord is moving in the United States, not just overseas. This is a time of visitation. It isn't just a "Holy Ghost Party" (although there is plenty of that going on). It is spreading into evangelism, spiritual growth, and discipleship. Now is the time to press in and seize the moment.

July 2, 2012—
Los Angeles

I went into the bank today, and the teller (a Muslim) asked me, "How was your weekend?"

"Hot," I replied. "I was in Dallas speaking at a church. However, it was worth it; a woman who had been deaf in her left ear for many years was healed." The teller stopped what she was doing and gaped at me. Her operations supervisor (also a Muslim) was also standing there, and she stopped what she was doing to look at me too.

"That is remarkable!" she said.

"Actually, we see it regularly," I told her. "Jesus is in the healing business, didn't you know that?"

"You must come in again and tell us more about this Jesus," she said. [The pair later came to a meeting I was leading in the area. One was born again, and the other still had questions.]

To be effective at evangelism, testimony matters. Most people need at least five testimonies before they come to faith. This was contact one of five. Check.

July 15, 2012—
Los Angeles

Last night we had a gathering for worship, teaching, and ministry at a church only a few miles from my home. Even though we were in Southern California, not Australia or Indonesia or some other exotic location, this meeting was amazing. People were being healed as they stood up to respond to words. A couple of them had the power of God hit them, and they just fell over healed without ever moving from their spot. It was a good thing that one of them had been sitting on a couch because she keeled over backward. The Lord touched many conditions, but the healings we could readily confirm without additional medical input included bladder problems, neuropathy, partial blindness caused by retinopathy, asthma, and some other unusual things that aren't easily categorized, like one woman who had scar tissue in her sinuses that kept her from breathing well. Her nose opened so she could breathe.

My eldest daughter was on fire last night; it seemed that every person for whom she prayed just collapsed under the anointing and was instantly healed. She was very excited.

Deliverance was going on all night long, but things ramped up around 11:30 p.m. I don't understand why it happens that way. (Does anyone remember the old Edgar Winter album *They Only Come Out at Night?*) Anyway, there was a lot of really deep and powerful deliverance. At one point a prayer team member and I were ministering to a woman, and it became clear that there was a demonic power tied to her, having previously been placed in a circle of candles. I and two of the other prophetic people present saw this. Nevertheless, I always like to confirm that such visions are based in objective reality, so I asked about what I was seeing. She acknowledged this had happened, then my prayer partner suddenly asked with great urgency (this was a manifestation of the gift of faith coming over her), "This was from Peru, wasn't it?!" The woman acknowledged that it was, whereupon my partner began addressing the demon in Spanish, her first language.

This was a powerful occultic spirit, somewhat akin to that of a *curandera*, yet different. (*Curandera* is a Spanish word for a woman who is a healer, often a shaman. *Curandero* is the male form.) As the woman manifested, her tongue stuck out and began wiggling and flailing like a serpent's. Nevertheless, Jesus was on the case, and with a cataclysmic power encounter, the spirit broke and left with a loud shriek. Everyone who was still there erupted into applause, laughter, thanksgiving, and rejoicing! This is as it should be when Jesus sets the captives free. Colossians 2:15 says that Jesus made a public spectacle (mockery) of evil spirits at the cross, and this was on full display last night. The woman afterward said she felt light and clean, she could breathe, and the pain/weight that had been on the left side of her chest for years was gone. It was awesome to see the freedom that this woman received last night! Glory to God!

Another very interesting deliverance was a well-dressed, well-educated woman who was a first-generation Christian from a Buddhist background. Yes, there were generational spirits. But there were also spirits that had come in during her non-Christian days when money was burned to provision ancestors for the afterlife, and another when she was angry with Christians for telling her she shouldn't be honoring her ancestors in such ways (this spirit was also causing an eye disease and advancing physical blindness); additionally, there was a Buddhist spirit, including spirits that had entered when she was in the Buddhist temple eating food sacrificed to Buddha and those that had entered as she listened to the bells and smelled the temple incense (i.e., the demonic power was tied to the sound of the bells, which I could clearly hear while we were praying for her, and to the incense that she breathed in, which I could distinctly smell while we were praying for her), and also spirits from new moon and full moon festivals. One of the more tenacious spirits was called "the moon god." [I know this may be stretch for you; for that I apologize. I try very hard not to overstate things nor get too far into the realm of the bizarre or unsubstantiated. However, I also like for these reports to be educational and to shift the paradigm many of us live in.]

These were all spirits we dealt with in this woman. They had been lying in the background, quiet yet still malicious. In war, bunkers (strongholds) need to be cleaned out, even after the invading army has swept across the land, and a bunch of them did get cleaned out last night.

One last deliverance pertains to a woman who had once used a Ouija board at a sleepover during her teen years. This woman is now in her twenties. She took pains to say that she had never dabbled in the black arts at any other time. Nevertheless, the spirits that had piled onto her were numerous and included divination, necromancy, clairvoyance, clairaudience, and some of the more "conventional" spirits such as shame, rejection, and bitterness.

Friends, please, please listen to the Lord and stay away from all of these practices such as visiting fortune-tellers, going to séances, and consulting card readers. I know of a group of very affluent and successful businesswomen in Orange County, California, who go out for a monthly girls' night, where they have dinner, wine, and maybe take in a movie. Recently, nearly twenty of them (some of whom purport to be Christians) went to a medium to have their cards read. The black arts have gone mainstream because the knowledge of the Lord, of His Word, and of His injunctions against such practices has passed from Western culture. Of the few who do know about them, some may dismiss them as belonging to the Old Testament and so no longer relevant. As the sailors of old used to say, "Danger! Thar be dragons!"

September 3, 2012—
Mandurah, Western Australia

The opening night of the conference was a great start to our meetings here. Our host church has a diverse worship team that did an impressive job last night. Partway through, there was a perceptible uptick in the intensity of the worship, accompanied by a burst of joy that rippled through the crowd. I didn't see or sense anything other than the presence of God, but Bruce reported seeing five angels walk in, and as it happened, one of them spread its wings over the room as we experienced that surge in the worship. [You can evaluate his report as you wish, but in any case, the upsurge in the worship was quite noticeable—and electrifying.]

After I finished speaking, the Holy Spirit moved through the room, and many people were touched powerfully. People crumpled onto the floor and onto the pews. The church looked like a battlefield, with bodies strewn about wherever they had fallen. Some bowed down as the power of God came over them. Several told me later they had not experienced His power in this fashion before. This is a classic "More, Lord!" situation, where the hunger of the people is attracting the presence of God. Incidentally, I felt an immediate kinship with this pastor and his wife, and I am looking forward to getting to know both of them better.

[One humorous healing involves a man who was sitting with his back to the central pillar supporting the roof. I could see that he had a significant problem with his neck, which appeared to be dystonia. I pointed at him and said, "Sir, the Lord is healing you." He replied, "I don't believe in these things." I repeated myself, as did he. I responded, "It doesn't matter whether you believe in these things—Jesus is healing you right now. Please get on your feet and come forward." So he did, but before he could reach me, the power of God hit him and he fell down. As he lay there on the floor, shaking, he continued to repeat, "I don't believe in these things." Afterward, when he had regained full mobility in his neck, he said again, "I don't believe in these things!" That man literally got healed against his will. Every so often, our Father has a sense of humor and literally puts on a show.]

September 7, 2012— Bunbury, Western Australia

Our last night in a town up the road was rather remarkable. The Holy Spirit began by falling on Bruce and Kathy and me while we were having tea with the pastors in a room just off the sanctuary.

Kathy was literally knocked to the floor, vibrating, interceding, and experiencing some kind of trance. She was unable to complete her meal, barely making it into the sanctuary for the start of the service more than an hour later. Meanwhile, Bruce managed to stay in his chair. However, he very nearly did a face-plant into his food while under the power of the Spirit. I fell into some kind of deep, resting reverie. None of this was planned or orchestrated, nor were we acting out in fleshly ways to get attention. It just happened. *Kaboom!*

Once we had pulled ourselves together to prepare for the night's meeting, a local prophetess and I had a few minutes of prayer, during which we both felt strongly that we should wait on the Lord after worship before I began to teach. I did this at about 8:20 p.m., and for the benefit of the uninitiated, I explained what we were doing and why. I then asked if anyone had a tongue that they had been afraid to give. One person offered a prophecy, which was good and quite anointed. Then we waited for the tongue. After a couple of long moments (less than a minute in fact, but it seemed longer because we were simply waiting in silence and silence tends to feel awkward), someone gave the tongue, and she was clearly not "making it up." It flowed out of her with that *nabi'* anointing and literally broke things loose in the room. [*Nabi'* is the Hebrew word for prophet and describes what happens when words come tumbling out of your spirit with power. It is kinetic. There are two other types of prophetic anointings—*ro'eh* and *hozeh*—which are more visionary, passive, and receptive.] I then asked for the interpretation, which came forth. I had my watch sitting on the podium to help me manage my speaking length, so I timed each part of what happened next.

At about 8:25 the Spirit began falling on the left side of the room, and several people were knocked to the floor. On the right side of the room, some people were looking frightened, so I explained to them that sometimes the Holy Spirit will differentially fall on a room. Usually, this is the start of a wider engagement that is about to happen. However, I invited anyone who wanted to relocate so they would be "closer to the spout where the glory's coming out" to do so. A few people immediately stood up and went over to the left. Several others cautiously followed behind, not sure what to expect.

About that time, I asked if anyone had any oil on their hands, and about a dozen people all over the room stood. I began walking around commenting on this phenomenon. The oil began to increase, and some were swept to the floor, while others simply crumpled in heaps. I laid hands on some, which visibly affected them and pushed their engagement with the Holy Spirit to higher levels.

At 8:28 the "Toronto Express Train" arrived. I almost hesitate to report this because what happened in Toronto still causes consternation for many Charismatics as well as virtually all non-Charismatics. [The Toronto Blessing was an outpouring of the Holy Spirit that began in 1994 and is characterized by laughter, a manifestation that frightens many Evangelicals because it looks chaotic, and they feel that God should always be orderly.] I didn't invite the present visitation, nor did I do anything to provoke it. It simply hit with so much power and force that it couldn't be contained. At precisely 8:28 a wave of laughter hit the room, engulfing several. They could not control themselves and literally just slid off the pews onto the floor or staggered around like drunks leaving the local pub at closing time. Some lost their footing, falling to the floor laughing. Some slumped together, attempting to hold one another up before falling down in heaps of laughter.

While this was happening, I invited anyone who wanted to participate in what the Lord was doing to come forward for prayer. Various people got up to do just that. Most never made it. As they were walking down the aisles, they were cut down by the power of God, almost as if one of the Vatican's Swiss guards had pole-axed them. Some of these lay under God's power for over an hour. Meanwhile, weeping and even (yes I admit it, with some trepidation) "roaring" broke out in the sanctuary. It was a bit chaotic, but it was organized chaos, orchestrated by the Holy Spirit with a little help from me (but not much). I must admit, it *did* look like Toronto all over again. I was both delighted and chagrined because I knew word of this would get out, and perhaps not with favorable results.

At about 8:38 I called four of the people with oil on their hands to come forward and help me pray for a boy with a human growth hormone deficiency. His mother stood for prayer with her son in her arms, and some kind of zone of power came over her, her son, and the four people who had come forward to assist with the prayer. The mother and her son were almost immediately overcome with the Spirit. This was not merely being slain in the Spirit but something more powerful and profound. Two of the four prayer partners were overloaded with the power of God, and they fell to the ground, looking as though they had been electrocuted. The look of shock and wonderment on the faces of the crowd said it all.

"And the power of the Lord was with Jesus to heal the sick" (Luke 5:17, NIV).

I love it when the Holy Spirit unleashes heaven in this way. He shows His sweet and loving nature, His tender compassion for the sick, wounded, and broken—all while displaying His zeal for His people. Healings began happening around the room, so we shifted into blessing what the Father was doing by praying for the sick and the injured. One woman came forward for prayer, and I asked how she was doing. She admitted that she was frightened and had run out of the meeting earlier when the other manifestations were happening, but one of the elders had brought her back and assured her it would be OK. With trepidation, she asked for prayer for a serious, crippling injury that kept her neck at an odd angle and without full mobility. I barely touched her before she was knocked to the floor. This wasn't merely being slain in the Spirit; it was more powerful than that. She lay on the floor for more than twenty minutes, but when she arose, she was fully healed. She was dumbfounded, having never experienced God in this way. Many others were healed during this short window of time.

About 9:08 I finally began to teach, and I finished my message on the signs of a Christian undergoing transformation in just under forty-four minutes. We then resumed ministry time at roughly 10 p.m. and didn't finish until after 1 a.m., finally returning home about 2 a.m.

September 10, 2012—
Perth, Western Australia

Yesterday I finished up five meetings on the kingdom of heaven in a regional center about two hours south of Perth. I hadn't taught a series on the kingdom in several years, so it was personally enriching to cover these "rules of the road" for kingdom living. One of my intercessors had sent me a message saying that getting to the point of breakthrough here would take some work, and this proved to be the case. Why this was so I haven't figured out. However, yesterday morning's ministry time got decidedly more powerful and "rambunctious."

I don't seek emotionalism in the meetings I lead, but I am conscious after years of experience that emotion (e.g., shouting, tears, laughter, jumping, and so on) often accompanies people receiving decisive touches from God. These touches are what I and others in this type of ministry call breakthrough. When this happens, I am always mindful that there may be those present who don't understand and may be frightened—those whom Paul calls the uninitiated (1 Cor. 14:16, 23).

I think we got through it all OK, but it was reminiscent of a Southern California Vineyard church some thirty-two years ago, also in a small town, where the Holy Spirit fell with great power. A certain pastor named John Wimber was overcome with anxiety about what had just happened. He went home and by his own testimony searched the Scriptures through the night, asking the Lord for wisdom. In the wee hours of the morning, a man called from Denver saying the Lord had awakened him and told him to call with this word: "John, it's OK. This is Me." I pray that if anyone was unduly rattled, the Lord will send just such a trusted friend to confirm to them the grace of God, even when it comes in an untidy package.

While I was in Perth, the Lord ministered to several who found breakthrough in the form of deep inner healing. One person had labored under a bondage to performance for years. Another had been anxious about money for many years. Another had a leadership calling on his life that he had been evading, and the Lord both addressed this and enlarged his capacity to receive the love of God. There was also a young girl from Zimbabwe who was quickly healed of complications from major abdominal surgery. The day after I ministered there, she was running around and playing as any child should. She and her mother were both delighted. Another woman who had sustained permanent damage to her back and lower spine due to severe beatings from her stepmother forty years earlier was also dramatically healed. Along with healing she received deliverance from several deeply entrenched spirits that had entered through the beatings. When we left yesterday, she was bending over, touching her toes, and smiling broadly. Even the shadow over her face was gone!

When I see healings of this type, I am often tempted to ask, "Why did it take so long for her to receive her healing?" Lacking complete answers to this question, I think the best course of action is to thank the Lord for His mercies poured out to those who receive and to continue asking for those who have yet to receive. Healing is available, but sometimes we need hidden keys to unlock it. This is why Jesus said, "I will give you the keys of the kingdom of heaven" (Matt. 16:19). Just so, there were a few who did not receive what they had hoped for during these meetings, but some of them will be joining us in the next town this coming weekend. I will be praying that the Lord touches them there.

September 18, 2012— Yallingup/Bunker Bay, Western Australia

Wagin is a small farming community in the interior of Southwest Australia, with fewer than ten thousand in the entire area. It lies thirty kilometers east of the Perth-to-Albany highway and has been a "crossing point" for centuries, going back to the time of the Aborginals' dominion over the area. Just so, people came to this meeting from Wagin, Narrogin (about sixty kilometers away), as well as from Lake Grace (Nice name, don't you think?) about one hundred sixty kilometers to the east, and even Esperance, over four hundred kilometers south on the southern coast of Australia. We also had several from the West Coast, from Bunbury, Australind, Mandurah, and Perth.

The Holy Spirit moved during our sessions, and a few things stand out in my mind. First, a couple who had come from Bunbury/Australind and were staying at the local caravan park started talking with a woman from Brisbane, on the opposite side of the continent. How she happened to be in this particular campsite in Wagin at this time was a divine appointment! They brought her along to the meetings, where she recommitted her life to Christ. As part of the package, the Lord unfroze/healed her C3/C4/C5 spinal fusion and healed/adjusted her lower back and hips so she could lie flat. These injuries were sustained twelve years previously when she hit a kangaroo with her car while driving in Queensland. She also got delivered of some things. She went home a very happy camper (pun intended)!

Another woman was healed of a tendon problem in her hip. It was some kind of degenerative disease, and when one of our teenage ministry team members, who happens to be wheelchair-bound and has tendon problems as a byproduct of his disease (for now), rolled up to pray for her, she crumpled to the ground and rose healed! She was delighted, and so was our young prayer minister.

A third story involves a man who had been brought from two hundred kilometers away. I saw him in the crowd wearing dark glasses (odd for an indoor meeting, I thought). These glasses had vision correction, but they were dark due to his acute light sensitivity. A member of the prayer team was praying for him when I walked up. As soon as I touched him, I knew he had served hard time. In fact, he had served more than twenty years in prison. He had been a bar and street brawler, and he had the physique to go with it.

He had been a Christian for some time, but he continued to struggle with his walk. The Holy Spirit came on him with great power, and he was delivered of many spirits, including one named "Fight." Before its eviction, he was moving around like a boxer, knocking chairs about, punching and growling. After it was over, his light sensitivity was *gone*! We tested this several times over two sessions, and he was totally healed. Just as important, he said that he felt internally free in ways he had never felt before. He recommitted his life to Christ on a deeper level with a new understanding of what this meant, and he had a feeling of peace that he had never known and a new reality of God in his life. [When I returned to that town the following year, he was not present—but his friends told me he sent his greetings, that all of his struggles in his walk with God had vanished, and he was now leading several Bible studies of his own.]

November 6, 2012—
Perth, Western Australia

Things are stirring here in an exciting, profound way. Churches are connecting with one another, including churches of various ethnic groups. It's a direct fulfillment of a word that was given to several of us last year by a prophet whom we regard highly. We weren't sure what the word meant at the time, but it is starting now, including over in the eastern states with some of the Aussies who are fellow travelers in the things of Spirit. Most notable is the move of God that is happening in Sydney among the Chaldeans (Iraqis) as reported by Jerry and others.

Among the linkages the Lord is creating here in the West, there are Anglican, Assemblies of God, Baptists, independent Pentecostals, Uniting Church, Vineyard, and ethnic churches that include Han Chinese, Iranian, Malaysian Chinese, Singaporean Chinese, and Indian. There are others, but this is enough to give a sense of the breadth of interconnection.

Yesterday afternoon, the Lord told me to change the message I had planned and to focus on leadership and the coming move of God. Shortly thereafter, I got several text messages from my friend Alfie in the United States, who had received some words from the Lord for me. He gave me several names of people who would be in the meetings that evening. First was a man named Joe. As it happened, the sponsoring pastor of the meeting was also named Joe, although he goes by Joey. You can't make this stuff up! Alfie also got the name "Edie" but wasn't sure if it was for a woman or a man (possibly Eddy or maybe Edith). These were people who had a profound call on their lives—even a destiny—to be part of what God is unleashing in the southwest of Oz. A few minutes later Alfie sent another message saying he was seeing a guy with a reddish color, perhaps reddish hair, and maybe a beard. A few minutes later he messaged again saying that he was getting the names

"Jimmy" and "Paul." (He said he knew it sounded hokey because now we had three names that sounded like a singing trio, but he was willing to go out on a limb because I was the one in Australia, not him. What would we do without our prophetic friends?)

After I finished the message last night, I shared the substance of the words Alfie had sent to me. I then called Joey up to the front, and I asked if there was a Paul in the room. It turned out there were *three* pastors named Paul in the room, one of them a woman named Paula. I then asked for Jimmy. Nobody responded at first, but there was a man seated in the back whom the Spirit had been pointing out to me all night. It turned out his name was Jimmy Mike, and he had a decidedly reddish complexion and a long white beard—he kind of looked like Billy Gibbons of ZZ Top. These five gathered at the front, and I felt led to pray for an impartation of leadership to steward the outpouring that is coming across Western Australia.

This initiated an outpouring of the Spirit that went on for well over an hour. Nearly every person in the room was hammered by the power of God, especially these ministers. A pastor named Eddie was also touched as well as several other pastors who simply hadn't been called by name from across the Pacific. The meeting wasn't that large, but we had a remarkable representation of pastors. This is consistent with the Spirit's leading on my sermon topic as previously mentioned and with the cross-linking of churches that is happening here in the West.

One of the men who came forward for prayer last night is a pastor named Larry. He had been a businessman before he was called by God to move to Western Australia to pray, prepare for, and participate in leading the move of God that is being birthed in the Southwest. Larry has *twice* been raised from the dead! During the weekend, I had said in one of my sermons that I was waiting for the Lord to begin raising the dead in our midst, and I took Larry's presence in the meeting last night as a sign that He heard me.

Larry is Indian, and he had just returned from a ministry trip to Singapore in which a woman in a wheelchair had gotten up during the sermon, totally healed. He has also experienced a wide range of unusual supernatural occurrences, which you might expect of someone who has been dead twice. He came forward to receive prayer from me, but I was hungry for what he had, so he also laid hands on me. I'm not sure who got more from whom, but I ended up on the floor for about twenty minutes while the Spirit continued moving through the room with great power. It was crazy! Larry and I are scheduled to meet tomorrow to talk about my next trip to Western Australia. The momentum is certainly here for a wider move of the Spirit, and he wants to join forces in extending this nascent awakening.

Last night's visitation would not have happened without a sure word of prophecy to initiate it and to provoke faith in the room. I often have people ask why we must have prophetic utterance in a move of God, and I tell them that the voice of prophecy awakens and incites the power of God. Many don't like prophetic utterance because it is "messy." Many others don't like the kinds of people who often prophesy, although mature prophets like Alfie don't typically have much social baggage. However, Scripture says, "Do not quench the Spirit. Do not despise prophecies, but test everything; hold fast what is good" (1 Thess. 5:19–21). One of the lessons that the Lord recently spoke to me is that we often quench the Spirit by despising prophetic utterance. We do this by despising the prophet or by viewing the way the Spirit affects the prophet as, shall we say, "unseemly," by not wanting to wrestle with the implications of the words that are given or by dismissing those words out of hand (i.e., forgetting them before the sound of the prophet's voice has left the room). If we want the power of God (the hand of God), we must first hearken unto prophecies (the voice of God). Why would He give us His hand if we will not listen to His voice?

Of course not all prophecies are of equal value. Some arise merely from good intentions (flesh) but don't have the breath of the divine upon them. Others are flat-out wrong. Some are false prophecies birthed with an intent to deceive (although these aren't in the majority). So none of what I am saying is a blanket endorsement of all prophecies, but it is to say that we must lean into prophecy as part of the widening move of the Spirit across our lands.

December 6, 2012— Bakersfield, California

When I got to the conference in Bakersfield, international prophet James Goll kicked things off by repeating large chunks of a conversation I had recently had with another leader about the growing move of God—a conversation about which I had not told him anything. In some cases, it was nearly verbatim. He had also had no contact with the other person. Need I say that God had my attention?

The messages of James and conference speakers Wesley Campbell, founding pastor of New Life Church in Kelowna, British Columbia, and Ché Ahn, pastor of Harvest Rock Church in Pasadena, California, built upon each other until the intensity of the Spirit was overwhelming. Suffice it to say I was captivated at every single session and overawed to hear of the many areas where the Lord is moving with great power. This includes a location in India that has historically been among the most resistant to the gospel and where Christians had represented less than 0.01 percent of the population. In this place, there have been 287,000 conversions in the last three years. Churches are being planted, and signs and wonders of a truly awesome magnitude are spreading. We learned of entire villages being converted in one meeting, limbs growing out, and numerous resurrections. Some missiologists are saying that this move of God should properly be called the Fourth Wave or the Third Great Awakening. There seems to be ample evidence to support these claims. In other words, *it has already begun*!

I was also privileged to attend a private dinner with these three speakers, and the level of connection we experienced was tremendous. I expect that several new doors will open for each of us from that one meal. I don't think saying it was a destiny-filled weekend would be an overstatement. It certainly was for me.

Destiny. There is that word again.

The world is changing; I feel it in my bones. Even if God isn't visiting your area yet, He will. Expect a divine summons. He is summoning all back to the front lines. We are crossing a line of demarcation. Lay down the white flags and pick up your weapons, the spiritual ones that have divine power to demolish strongholds. Determine to press into spiritual maturity. Soon the cries of "We want the King to return! We want the King to return! We want the King to return!" will be echoing through the earth, then He will appear, riding a white horse with the armies of heaven behind him.

PILLAR 3

Power

*The tree is known by its fruit. You brood of vipers!
How can you speak good, when you are evil? For out of
the abundance of the heart the mouth speaks. The good
person out of his good treasure brings forth good, and
the evil person out of his evil treasure brings forth evil.*
—MATTHEW 12:33–35

EOPLE OFTEN ASK me how they can get more spiritual power. The hard but simple truth is that power and purity are intimately connected. What is the condition of your heart? The easiest way to find out is to check what is coming out of your mouth.

Jesus said, "Out of the abundance of the heart the mouth speaks" (Matt. 12:34). If the abundance in our hearts is good, then blessing, praise, and joy will come out of our mouths. If the abundance in our hearts is not good, then cursing, criticism, and anger will come forth. Jesus goes on to say that the good person brings forth good things from the good treasure of his/her heart, but the evil person brings forth evil treasure from the evil in his/her heart (Matt. 12:35).

Simply put, "You will know a tree by its fruit" (Matt. 7:16, 20; 12:33). "Inspecting fruit" has a long and negative connotation in many churches as it can look suspiciously like criticism, control, manipulation, and even self-exaltation. "Inspecting fruit" is nearly always directed at others with the intention of belittling and ruining them. Yet we are not called to tear others down; we are called to build them up. So instead of spending energy to search out "hypocrites," why not turn the spotlight on ourselves?

What is the abundance in your heart that flows out of your mouth? Do you even know?

The Puritans called the practice of inviting the Holy Spirit to turn his light on us "The Prayer of Examen." As the psalmist wrote, "Search me, O God, and know my heart; test me and know my anxious thoughts" (Ps. 139:23, NLT). Of course, praying this way can be risky. The Holy Spirit may show us things we would rather not see, things we can hardly believe are in us.

I had an experience like this a few years ago in which I learned, much to my dismay and embarrassment, that I was often harsh and impetuous, despite my best intentions not to be this way. Some may protest in my defense that my intentions were good and therefore the fruit should be counted as good. However, such is not the case. Good intentions do not guarantee good outcomes. The Bible says that we prove our faith (favorable thoughts and intentions) by our works (how we live outwardly) (Jas. 2:18).

Though we may try to convince ourselves that good intentions are enough, Scripture reminds us that "the heart is deceitful above all things" (Jer. 17:9). When God showed me my failings in this area, I wept for weeks. Part of this was grief and godly sorrow; some of it was sheer embarrassment; some of it was a cry for mercy. In time the Lord helped me change my ways, but even to this day, I remain vigilant lest I fall into old patterns once again.

Every so often, we need wives or husbands, children or coworkers, friends or fellow church members, or eventually pastors to point these things out to us since we may be spiritually blind. In fact, we most likely *are* spiritually blind. When we can receive this input without reacting angrily or sulking, we will know we are starting to grow spiritually.

So where does this leave us? We can only know the state of

our hearts by examining what flows out from our lives: our attitudes, speech, body language, facial expressions, and tone of voice. What is your abundance? Clearly seeing the answer to this question and responding to it is a key to entering the deeper life.

March 3, 2013—
Los Angeles

I am home once again and reflecting on the ministry trip I just took to Australia. It was great, and in parts of it I saw more blessing and outpouring, more power, and more overt healing and deliverance than I have seen in twenty-five years. I know that is a big statement, but it is true. Best of all the Australian outpouring is now flowing well in many denominational streams, including Anglican, Baptist, Foursquare, independent Pentecostal, and even in the Uniting Church! We had a chance to interact with all of these and a couple of Vineyard churches on this trip.

Everywhere I went throughout the Sydney and Adelaide metropolitan areas, I saw a groundswell of interest among people and leaders for a deep move of God accompanied by powerful preaching of the Word and signs and wonders. At nearly every meeting, people gave their lives to Christ for the first time. Australia is heating up!

I taught on evangelism at a Vineyard church near Sydney, and the impartation of the Holy Spirit that came was beautiful and powerful and brought many to tears. The next Sunday morning, the Lord had prophetic words for each of the children of the church. The looks and exclamations of surprise that came from the parents' mouths spoke profoundly about how accurately the Holy Spirit was speaking to these children about their present lives and their future destinies.

Some of the healings we saw on this trip were just breathtaking. In response to a word of knowledge given at one of the Baptist churches, a man came up for prayer, not really sure if he believed in healing. When his tumors completely dematerialized—his wife felt his abdomen and confirmed that they were gone—he was at a total loss for words. I have since heard from his wife, and the tumors are still gone. For the record, we know from prior medical information that they were benign, but even benign tumors can turn malignant sometimes, so it's better not to have them—or so Jesus apparently thought. We also saw Jesus finish out a couple of healings from the last trip as well as many healings of arthritis and mobility impairments of all kinds.

These meetings set a new high-water mark for the outpouring of the Spirit in Australia. The pastors created an environment in which the Holy Spirit had complete freedom to the point where a sweet, scented manifestation of Jesus' presence filled the room, much to everyone's delight. Sean had asked me to teach on "taking ground," which was a euphemism for deliverance, and all I can say is that the kingdom of heaven took a *lot* of ground back from the kingdom of darkness. Again I have not seen impartation this profound in at least twenty years, possibly longer; at times it was even a bit shocking to witness the Holy Spirit's raw power.

During ministry time, one of the team (the wife of an Anglican prelate!) was working with a demonized woman who was putting her hands over her ears and yelling repeatedly, "No, I'm not coming out! I'm not leaving! I can't hear you!" At this, nearly everyone in the church broke into laughter, but the prayer team leader pressed the attack and prevailed. The woman gave public testimony in front of the church the next day to being freed of panic so profound that she could hardly leave her home to go shopping—for thirty years. How cool is that?! At another point, I was teaching on how to get demons out, and a woman in the foyer (narthex) was growling and howling and screaming so loudly that it served as sound effects for the very things I was teaching. Sean and those with him also saw that spirit and its companions vanquished in the name of Jesus.

It seemed that the conference opened a deep well for central South Australia. Afterward, I got a message from the pastor of a Baptist church several hundred kilometers away. He had come to the conference skeptical but was powerfully touched by God.

He wrote to say that the Holy Spirit fell on his church the day after he returned, with over a half-dozen people healed on the spot (most subsequently confirmed), and one person delivered of evil spirits. I was especially blessed to hear this because it shows that what is happening is being carried away and freeing others. This is exactly as I have taught in my message on how to propagate a revival (which covers Paul's Ephesian ministry as described in Acts 19). This outpouring is contagious, and it is going viral! Bring it on!!!! God is on the move!

April 9, 2013— Los Angeles

Things are popping here in SoCal. On Sunday night, I spoke in the Los Angeles South Bay region on "Moves of God." We had a lengthy ministry time at the end, and the Holy Spirit moved dramatically. It was one of those nights where our Father allows His Spirit to be called down upon people from some distance away. As a result, daisy chains of the Lord's smitten ones made lines across the room. One man was hit so hard by the Holy Spirit he was blown backward and continued to slide backward for several feet on the carpeted floor after he landed. It was crazy and wonderful and awe-inspiring. My thanks to the pastor for the invitation and for his openness to the Spirit. Without that freedom, nights like Sunday don't occur.

Last night I was in Long Beach for the conclusion of a twelve-week training series on healing. I felt prompted to share some material on forgiveness that I have not taught for many years. It was one of the most powerful nights I have seen in a long, long time. But this wasn't the same visual display of raw power as the previous one. Instead, this was a move of holiness.

It started when I invited the group to give prophetic words, asking those who had been flowing in words of knowledge and prophecy to please hold back so others could take a turn. First up was a word about someone who needed to forgive siblings. Then a sixteen-year-old boy said God wanted to touch those who needed to forgive parents. What followed was beyond words: The Holy Spirit descended in power, and all over the room, people began weeping, sobbing, screaming, finding release from things long forgotten (and in some cases, things that are unforgettable). I said, "You are about to have an encounter with the Trinity; the Father is here, reconciling you to Himself by the power of the Spirit and calling you to let your sins go into the hands and side of Jesus." I quoted Isaiah 53:4–6, emphasizing that it is by Christ's wounds that we are healed. I began to weep as an ever-increasing intensity of God's holiness filled the room; it was almost suffocating.

Something perceptibly shifted. As events started to unfold, I asked that we collectively honor an old rule: "What is shared here stays here." All agreed, and I too was bound by this. I will say, however, that people began to stand up and voluntarily confess unspeakable things—over the microphone! These weren't confessions of drunkenness or smoking. This was far, far deeper, darker, and more hidden stuff. Some sins were current, others from years ago. Many unburdened themselves of sins committed against them, both recently and in the past. I emphasize, these were things you would normally *never* hear admitted in any public setting, perhaps not even in a private counseling or prayer setting, and certainly *not* in front of the church.

Smoldering embers of agony, which for years had episodically leaped into tortured flames—things that had driven the people of faith to despair and unspeakable shame—were quenched in the waters of Shiloh.

It reminded me of the old-time revival meetings where people would stand and confess their sins, then stream forward to fall on their faces, weeping and seeking forgiveness, only to rise from the "mourner's bench" free, saved, and holy. Thus, the spirit of liberty came!

Men and women were being unshackled as the power of heaven descended. Deliverance broke out, including deliverance from words and curses pronounced by pastors and parents that had quenched the life of God in people for decades. Three times I tried to close the service, and He would not let me. People continued to confess and receive ministry from the body as prayer circles formed around them. It was stunning.

At one point a woman was receiving prayer, and another woman walked up to me and said, "I think I need to open the back door, and we all need to yell, 'Get out' [to the spirit that was manifesting]." This is *not* "normal" white middle-class church behavior! But the woman walked to the back, opened the door, and we *all yelled*, "Get out!" The woman receiving prayer pitched forward, coughing, hacking, manifesting...and rose up free! Nearly three decades of being caught in a spiritual vise was over. Then she experienced a wave of healing for a condition she'd had for years.

Friends, something has shifted. God is moving in Southern California, and based on calls I've gotten from Europe this week, it is happening more widely. This is more than a wave; it is a tsunami. Church, will you not perceive it? The tide is rising rapidly.

April 28. 2013— Canberra. Australian Capital Territory

The last three days have been both fun and amazing. I was with a good-sized group of *switched-on* Anglicans at Spirit '13, a renewal event in coastal New South Wales. Not only did the Lord confirm His Word, but He gave me tremendous grace in proclaiming it, which the participants received with great gladness (Mark 4:16; Acts 17:11). I wish I always spoke with such clarity!

The Lord was extremely gracious and allowed great prophetic

accuracy to flow from the platform on Saturday afternoon. He also moved in a mighty way when we laid hands on people for empowerment and impartation. I could tell many stories, but one that is both interesting and humorous occurred on Saturday night.

We had gone to dinner at a local restaurant, and as we sat at a table, I was telling stories of God's dealings in Whyalla in February. Next to me was a woman from Whyalla, and as I described the great move of God and the deliverance many experienced there, she began manifesting in the restaurant and pitched forward onto her face! Luckily we moved the plate of food before she landed in her dinner! Plenty of eyes were open wide, and not just at our table. I had food in my mouth at that moment, so I kept chewing, but I put my hand on her back, as did the woman on her other side. After I swallowed my food, I rebuked the spirit and told it to come out, which it did with coughing and some mild shouting. This *really* got people's attention. When it was over, we all resumed our meal. Ho-hum, just another dinner with Jesus at the table!

My friends, when demons are cast out by the finger of God, even in the middle of dinner at a restaurant, then know with certainty that the kingdom of God has come among you (Luke 11:20)!

May 1, 2013—
Young, New South Wales, Australia

The meeting last night was well attended, especially for a weeknight in a small country town. This is the cherry capital of Australia, and it is beautiful country, though experiencing a dry spell. Autumn is in the air, and the few deciduous trees in the area are aflame with color.

The pastor asked me to speak on something that would encourage and strengthen the church, so I spoke on healing being the children's bread and how we should expect God to heal us when we ask. The Lord graciously touched people, including a couple with skeletal problems in their feet and others with urinary conditions and migraines. Two people came forward with chronic, life-threatening conditions; one was a woman whose kidneys had "died." While I was speaking, she felt extreme heat go through her body, especially her back, and heard a voice in her head urging her to go forward for prayer. The Spirit of God came on her visibly when she did, and she said that the various severe pains throughout her body left. It is too early to say her kidneys came back to life, but *something* clearly happened to her. I hope to get a more thorough report before we leave here on Friday.

Often healings of this type will cause people to respond in awe and thereby make changes in their lives they previously would not have been open to making.

There is a great need for unity among the churches in Young, and I pray that our visit here will be the start of it. In my travels, I visit many churches and meet many pastors. It disturbs me to see the church in this land and in the United States riven with disputes and debates about things that are clearly settled in Scripture. How can we advance when we are confused about the "main and the plain" things of Scripture?

I increasingly see the need for the church to return to a rock-ribbed confidence in and proclamation of the Bible as the infallible Word of God. I know for some readers that sounds too far to the right and perhaps even "fundamentalist" (in all the wrong ways), but the reality is that if the church doesn't teach, preach, and hold to the truths of Scripture, nobody else will—not the Muslims (they have the Qu'ran), not the Buddhists, not the Hindus (they have the Vedas), not the secularists, nobody. If the church loses the Scriptures, it will go out of business as surely as General Motors would if it stopped making automobiles.

Every great move of God in history has been strongly centered on the Word. Such moves did not seek to reinterpret Scripture but rather to reapply it to the times. During the reform of Josiah, the Bible (what of it existed at that time) was rediscovered and read publicly to the people (2 Kings 22). Ezra did the same thing after the exiles of Israel returned from captivity (Neh. 8). In both cases, the people of God had forgotten, lost, and wandered from the truths of Scripture. They were instantly struck with grief over all the ways they had violated God's Word once they heard it.

In God's mind, however, ignorance of the Scripture was no excuse for not following it. This is clear from the way the prophets spoke during these periods. Moreover, God's people clearly understood this, based on the way they responded to the reading of the Word. (Just read the two passages I have cited to see this for yourself.) Until the Word was rediscovered, we might say that the people of God were "making it up as they went along" because they were simply no longer grounded in the actual book itself. John Wimber used to say, "I'm like a sieve; I leak." We all leak, and we all drift from living the life God intended. We all need the plumb line of the Word of God to be held up so we can conform our minds and our lives to it, rather than living in whatever way seems appropriate for the age in which we live.

At one time, the church and Western civilization were so intertwined that it was not always easy to tell one from the other. Those days are long gone. The political, business, educational, and media leaders of the West despise the church, and the West's values, customs, and mores increasingly diverge from biblical norms and patterns. Unless we preach the Bible with confidence, that will not change. "And how are they to hear without someone preaching" (Rom. 10:14)?

What does any of this have to do with Young, New South Wales? Only that everywhere I go, I encounter people who are confused about truth and perplexed and vexed by the rising iniquity surrounding them.

While I was in Canberra earlier this week, I did an interview with a local Christian radio station. When we finished, the broadcaster began mourning the state of local affairs and describing the weaknesses of the churches in the city. In so many words, he described people in that region as suppressing "the truth by their wickedness" (Rom.1:18, NLT) and passing legislation to enshrine it.

Now I am in Young, which is anything but Canberra. Small towns have historically been bastions of religious devotion, slower to throw off traditional understandings, and especially those based in Scripture. Yet even here, the signs of spiritual torpor are evident. The disunity of the churches is just one metric of that. God has called us, the people of God, to ignite brushfires of spiritual awakening. With His help, we will do so, in the cities and the towns, in the highways and the byways. The hour is late, but it is not too late.

Jesus said, "I have come to set the world on fire, and I wish it were already burning" (Luke 12:49, NLT)! Indeed. Lord, let your fire touch the earth!

August 6, 2013—
Adelaide, South Australia

It has been a very satisfying time here, connecting with old friends and meeting new ones. I've led four sessions at a church. All were good, but the last was amazing.

We had a massive move of the Spirit, during which I felt led to call people forward for a release of revelation/wisdom/prophetic gifting rather than the traditional "empowering." The pastor's wife ended up on the floor for more than ninety minutes, laughing and giggling and rolling around (i.e., being a "holy roller"). Her husband said he had not seen her touched by God like that since 1995. There were also plenty of tears (good ones) and quite a few deliverances, some of them rather loud.

One of my favorite things involved a woman in her midtwenties who asked for prayer over her gluten intolerance. She could not eat without getting severe pain and was unsure how she was going to manage going forward. The Lord set her free of that condition. The next day, she reported that she had eaten a hamburger *with* a bun without side effects! That evening, she ate an entire pizza, again without side effects! The Lord touched several other areas too, and as the pastor's wife said when it was all done, "She has a new life!" It was whimsical, powerful, joyful, and heartwarming all at once.

I also spoke at another church this weekend, which likewise had a powerful move of the Spirit. Before the message, I was asked to pray for the children, and the spirit of prophecy came into the room such that each child received a prophetic word. Some were as young as three or four years old. The parents and people in the room who knew the children confirmed the parts of the words that pertained to who they are today, while those parts that dealt with future things remain to be weighed and tested. Do not hesitate to release prophecy over children. It will call them into their destinies. (See, for example, Paul's words to Timothy in 1 Timothy 1:5–6, 18.) Something about that time also stirred the adults to a newfound hunger for a move of God, and this included the elders. We had a luncheon after the service, and I prayed over the leadership team, nearly all of whom ended up wiped out in the Spirit, weeping, calling out to God, and the like. You know, just your typical after-church potluck at the manse.

Last night we had a wonderful session about recovering our first love and sustaining continuous revival for a lifetime. It occurred at a Baptist church that sits in the hills above Adelaide and has a long, storied history with the things of the Spirit that dates back to the Charismatic outpouring of the 1970s. Many people who attend there today were part of that move of God half a century ago, although the church as a whole is far from an aged congregation. The pastor loves the things of and holds earnestly to all that is best in the Baptist tradition, especially its focus on God's Word. He has become a dear and trusted friend over the last couple of years.

I was especially moved last night to see the Spirit powerfully touching more men than women during the ministry time, even ending up in tears of renewal and consecration. This is not to say that many women weren't also touched, nor is it to say that when women are touched, this is somehow less important. It is to say that during my travels, women more commonly respond to the Spirit and are therefore most powerfully touched. So to be in a church where the men were also being touched both widely and powerfully spoke volumes about the leadership and gave me hope that this really is a season where we are "all in."

August 9, 2013—
Young, New South Wales

The meetings in Young were not particularly large, but they were well attended given that this is a country town. The first meeting saw many people touched by the Holy Spirit, with around half ending up on the floor. Last night, however, was different.

After I preached, I had people break up into pairs for prophetic prayer. Then I asked each person to call forth the kingdom of God within his or her partner (Jesus said the kingdom of God is within you). I have never done this before, but I had had a vision of people praying in pairs and summoning the kingdom forth so it would come to the people. Individuals all over the room were touched—some crying, some laughing, some shaking or falling to the floor. For many of those praying, it was their first time to either give a prophetic word or see someone touched by the power of the Holy Spirit. I told them this was a dry run in a safe environment for what they could do in the shops, at school or work, and so on. After that we called all the sick to come for prayer (without any words of knowledge).

Many of the people who came for healing were powerfully touched. The team and I prayed for a man with osteoarthritis, which had disabled him and given him a hunched back. As a result, he was having difficulty breathing. The Lord touched him dramatically, such that on a scale of one to ten, his breathing difficulty dropped from ten to a one or zero. He also had significant pain throughout his body that limited mobility in his back, arms, hands, knees, and ankles; but after prayer he went home pain free for the first time in many years. To be clear, he still needs the deformities in his body healed, but this was a start and something he had never experienced!

We also prayed for a young man with cerebral palsy who had muscles hard as a rock from the stiffness and painful spasticity that is common to the condition. After prayer his hips loosened considerably, and he was able to bend his knees (something he could not do when he came to the meeting), swivel his feet (also something he could not do previously), and perform other manual tasks. He *also* began walking with some assistance, and the more we prayed for him, the less help he needed. As you might imagine, he was pretty blown away. That man needs more prayer to complete his healing, but he is well on the way, and he has experienced the reality of the kingdom of God in a way he had not dared to believe could happen for him. One line from him is worth quoting, "I'm liking this a *lot!*"

"So there was much rejoicing in that city" (Acts 8:8, NASB).

[After returning to Los Angeles, I received near-daily updates from this young man—each detailing further healing in his body every night as he lay on his bed. By the fourteenth day, he was completely healed. This fulfilled a prophetic word I had given him before the meeting began, not knowing what I was saying: I told him nonbelievers would come to him asking for his testimony.

As a result of this healing, many acquaintances at his university asked him what had happened. They could not understand how a man with cerebral palsy could now walk around without assistance. So the Lord not only healed him, He used him as a sign and a wonder too.]

September 20, 2013—
Perth, Western Australia

We have covered more than two thousand of the three thousand kilometers of this trip. We finished up in Esperance on Monday, then traveled through the rain to Bunbury on Tuesday. Before leaving Esperance, a few of us met with local church leaders; the Lord not only gave us prophetic words for them but also used them to give several unusual and exciting words to us. I think of how the apostle Paul wrote to the Romans that we are to mutually encourage one another with our faith (Rom. 1:12).

A teenage girl with dyslexia was healed; this was tested and confirmed. Throughout the rest of the day, this young woman kept giving me signs indicating that she was still healed and able to read her Bible along with me as I taught. I love it! Her mother was touched powerfully by the Spirit too, then she turned around and began praying for others. In that meeting we also saw a knee, shoulder, and at least two deaf people healed; one of the deaf people came back to the evening session without hearing aids. A man paralyzed due to a stroke three years ago was almost completely healed. His speech was about 75 percent restored, and otherwise he seemed to be back to normal—and quite happy about it. Since he is known to the organizers of the Bunbury meetings, he will hopefully get additional ministry and be 100 percent back to normal soon. His wife and son watched as he was being healed, alternating between disbelief, joy, and tears.

Last night I taught at a ministry school that draws people from several churches in Perth, including Baptists, Assemblies of God, Foursquare, independent Pentecostal, Uniting, and even a couple from liturgical traditions. I taught on tongues and interpretation of tongues. It is unusual these days for anyone to teach in depth about these two gifts, but when we had ministry time last night, the Lord really backed it up. Nearly everyone in the room came forward for ministry. All were filled with the Spirit and spoke in tongues or new tongues, received prayer so they could interpret tongues, or began moving in prophecy.

Following the activation, the Spirit moved in the room with several tongues given and interpreted. After each interpretation, I asked if others had also received interpretations of the tongues, and in general two to four others had received the same interpretation. Often people will speak in tongues when the Spirit arrives, but interpretation of tongues is far less common. So the Spirit was moving to balance these two gifts, which should operate as a pair. Prophecy was also stirred up as these tongues were given and interpreted. Through it all the Spirit was speaking a common theme: "Now is the time!" "Arise!" "The Lord is with you!" "God is calling Western Australia to awaken!" "The Lord is rebuilding His scattered army!" "The Lord is weaving a fabric of His people, knitting together what has come unraveled." It was inspiring, and it quickened me personally because I had not shared what the Lord has laid on my heart concerning this hour and this geographic region. However, through the combination of tongues, interpretation, and prophecy, the Lord delivered the message anyway.

Afterward, people told me they had never seen tongues given so clearly, decently, and in order. They had never seen them interpreted so well, with such confirmation from the room that these words were, in fact, from God, or seen such unity of theme and message in tongues, interpretation, prophecy, and so on. It seemed that yet again the Lord was recovering and re-establishing long-dormant gifts and stirring up those that may have fallen from favor. We need all the gifts (tools) of the Spirit to carry out the work of God, so I was happy to see the Lord stirring up the church in this way.

September 23, 2013—
Perth

This swing through the Southwest is nearly over. We finished up at Churchlands last night, and this morning we leave for Albany/Mount Barker, Western Australia. These are small, out-of-the-way places; though some well-known apostolic leaders have encouraged me to concentrate only on the metropolitan areas, the Word says Jesus went out into "the highways and byways"—and I feel this unction very keenly in my spirit as well.

The Churchlands crew is a hungry lot and was receptive both to the messages and to the ministry. Last night, some came forward for healing of blood conditions. One person was someone for whom one of my intercessors had received words of knowledge nearly a week earlier when he was praying and shared with me. He had never met this woman and had no way of knowing who would be at the meeting—and in fact he was in a completely different country. But his word of knowledge even included the name of her condition! Needless to say, when she heard it, her faith soared through the roof, then her body crashed to the floor as the power of the Spirit came over her. We also had a woman with a rare clotting disorder, which had caused her to have numerous strokes (both large and small). This disorder was caused by her grandfather's Freemason history, and once we dealt with that, she received healing power. The Holy Spirit touched her eye, healing about 95 percent of the blindness caused by the most recent stroke. The only thing that remained was a spot through which she could perceive light but where the image was "smudged," in her words. God is good, and I pray that He finished her healing overnight.

September 25, 2013— Albany, Western Australia

On our first night the meeting was small, with our team from Perth comprising a meaningful percentage of the crowd. But good things happened. Two people got saved, and two others rededicated their lives to the Lord. A woman was healed of carpal tunnel syndrome, and one man was healed of a shoulder condition he'd had since the Vietnam War.

In Mount Barker last night we also had a modest crowd. During the ministry time, a woman with a twisted, shriveled leg came forward to be healed. She had contracted polio at age two, something that is rarely heard of anymore. I prayed for her briefly, then left her with the team. The healing was nearly complete when we left the church, and it continued through the night. [When I returned to Albany a year afterward, in 2014, the woman was completely healed and walking normally.] On the same night the woman was healed, a man was healed of a shoulder and lower-back condition and also relieved of some "hitchhikers."

That night a woman also brought up her three-year old grandson, who was severely delayed in speech and development, nearly mute and with auditory processing disorder. I had him look into my eyes, then I quietly rebuked the spirit of muteness and asked the Lord to release healing over him. Within a few moments he looked at his mother and said, "Mum," then at his stepfather and said, "Dad." When he looked at me I asked if he could give me a high-five, which he did. Then he said, "Bye!" I asked his parents and grandmother if he could do this normally, and they said, "Occasionally." I deemed this inconclusive. Later in the evening as we were about to leave, his grandmother ran back into the church and exclaimed joyfully that the boy was talking, and she specifically mentioned that he had addressed someone named "Mike" by name. I didn't see him again, as he was already in their car ready to depart, but I took this to be a very good development.

It was a physically demanding trip, and I could not help but think how I would be feeling if, like Francis Asbury or John Wesley, we had traveled on horseback—especially in the wind and the rain. Many have questioned why we go to smaller towns like these in a sparsely populated region like Southwest Australia. The simplest answer is that it seems to be what the Holy Spirit is prompting.

More broadly, however, I remember a class on missions I took while in seminary. Paul Pierson, then dean of the School of World Mission [now the School of Intercultural Communication] at Fuller Seminary, laid out several common principles of historic moves of God. One was that they normally arise on the "edge," in unnoticed places. Rarely do they emerge "in the thick of things." For example, no great moves of God have arisen from Rome or Canterbury or for that matter, from Springfield, Missouri. Instead, they have arisen in off-the-beaten path places like Nazareth, Capernaum, Dublin, Assisi, Los Angeles, Costa Mesa, and Yorba Linda. At the time when each of those moves occurred, they were all in small, backwater, sleepy towns. As these moves of God expanded, "headquarters" jumped in—denominational leaders, local church leaders, or even people from overseas who felt they had a stake in what was going on—sometimes to bless and other times to control.

This morning, as I was driving back to Perth, I received a text from one of the "expectant ones" who lives in the West. She had attended a meeting in Perth last night in which a visiting minister from overseas had declared that a visitation was coming upon Western Australia, fulfilling prophetic words that had often been forgotten. He mentioned some of the same words I have referenced. She asked if he and I had the same notes (we didn't, as I had never heard of this man). She also said he had declared it has already begun.

Perhaps this is true, or perhaps we will wait still longer. Only time will tell. What I know is that expectation is in the air all throughout the West. Moreover, on this trip alone we saw one blind person, at least three deaf people, one partial paralytic, several mobility-impaired people (including bone-on-bone conditions and arthritis, knees, and shoulders and backs), at least one wheat allergy, several severe cases of PMS, apparently one polio victim with a twisted leg, and a learning-delayed person who could not speak—and all were touched by the power of God. My greatest disappointment is that due to my own fatigue I did not pray for as many as usual, and I wonder how much more could have happened. The people of the Southwest are awakening to the fact that God has not forgotten them or left them in their current state. The kingdom of heaven is at hand! Prepare the way of the Lord! Make straight paths for Him! I don't understand exactly where it is going or how soon we will get there; nevertheless, I too am expectant.

September 25, 2013— Qantas Flight 598 (Perth to Brisbane)

I have not been in Indonesia for two weeks, yet I am only now finishing my report on the trip to Papua.

Lobo was probably so named by Portuguese explorers (*lobo* means "large dog" or "wolf" in Portuguese) because of a local belief in a powerful doglike spirit called Swawu—the spirit ruler over Swangi. Whenever Swawu would come, all the dogs would howl and bark, but this spirit was dealt a decisive blow in February 1985 when the Spirit of God sovereignly fell on this small settlement without a missionary or minister ushering it in, resulting in disabled people being healed, people receiving the gift of tongues, a tree that Swawu lived under toppling(!), all the pigs running off, and a fire in the sky so intense it took two hours for the flames to dissipate. The next day the visitation ended, and since that time nobody has spoken in tongues. We interviewed four eyewitnesses to all of this on video; there are photos of the monument to this visitation that the villagers built. I was moved to tears as I reflected that the Lord had sovereignly come to this tiny village at the end of the earth more than twenty-eight years earlier to bless His people who were cut off from the outpourings of Azusa Street and beyond.

We spent one day in Lobo. There were no phones nor running water, only a generator that produced just enough electricity for the government-run clinic. Toilets were standard Indonesian issue, which means they were of the "squat" variety. A dirt road ringed the settlement, and two "streets" (footpaths really) ran through it. That night in the church where we gathered, the Spirit descended three times, with nearly all (perhaps all) of the villagers once again speaking in tongues.

The people had built a shelter next to the church for traveling ministers, boat captains, and other wayfarers. We slept there on mattresses thrown on the tile floor—the men in one room and the women in another. The next morning we rose and put to sea at first light to beat a rising swell and an incoming storm back to Kaimana.

When we arrived in Kaimana on September 5, we rested, checked out what local color we could find, and napped. On the main road, which snakes its way along the coast, we discovered concrete emplacements left from the Japanese occupation. These formerly held the shore batteries that rained down destruction on Allied ships that ventured too close to the harbor. We had seen similar remnants of the war last year on Biak, and it reminded me yet again that we are genuinely engaged in a spiritual war and that the battle lines sometimes run right through our midst.

That night, a local government official hosted an interdenominational service at his residence, which was high in the rainforest-clad hills above Kaimana, overlooking the sea. Stanley preached, and the Spirit touched people through his message. At dinner with the government official afterward, we prayed for some of the staff and guests. This bothered a few of the city elders, who thought that such things should neither happen in the leader's residence nor in his presence. Nevertheless, he invited us back the following morning for a private meeting, during which we prayed for him and spoke some prophetic words that seemed to find their mark. One included a lengthy word of wisdom on dealing with the Islamic insurgency on his island by healing an imam's daughter. (After he acted on that word, the insurgency dropped to zero.) Another involved deciding between two economic development proposals. The Lord allowed us to describe both proposals without anyone else telling us about them, and He released His wisdom on which was the better path. [In the years following, great economic prosperity flowed to that region because the official followed the Lord's direction.]

The local leader later told us that he had also been healed during the private meeting. We found favor with him, and he underwrote nearly all of the expenses for our time on Kaimana. Between food, gasoline, boats, and soldiers for protection (due to Muslim unrest), this was not an insignificant amount. He also met us at the airport as we were leaving the next day; he prayed with us and for us. It reminded me very much of Paul's visit to Malta, another island many miles and many lifetimes distant.

God blessed our last night in Kaimana, and two disabled people were healed in the service. One was a woman who had visited another town as part of a women's team from the church. While there, she had injured her foot, leaving her in excruciating pain. She had been this way for a month. Her healing required evicting some spirits, including a water spirit and a spider spirit.

It took about three and a half hours, including some prayer for healing at the mayor's home the night before, but it was worth the effort. When we left Kaimana, her husband came to the airport to bring me a new batik shirt as a gift and told me his wife was moving normally again that morning, cooking, caring for the children, and living life. That shirt is now my favorite.

[As for the spider spirit I mentioned, it looked like a large spider attached to her. As I was praying for her, my eyes were open, and I could see it on her leg. The water spirit came from a well she had walked past; others had warned her not to go near it because there were spirits attached to it, and she had said something to the effect of, "I am the righteousness of Christ, and nothing can harm me"—which is a common idea among Christians. But it's one thing to walk in that authority, and something else to say it because someone else taught you to say it. Sometimes people grab hold of concepts in faith, but in our day, people hear lots of teaching and decide to do things they don't actually have faith for. We must own our faith, establish boundaries, and walk in it consistently. Faith is not just "believeism" or mental agreement; it is confidence. You get to the place where you say, "The Lord has shown Himself to be faithful to me in this area so far, so why would He let me down now?" *That* is what faith is.]

The other disabled woman who was healed had come in on a cane. As the service was closing, she left the cane behind in the church and walked out.

From Kaimana, we flew to Nabire, a much larger town facing north on the Gulf of Papua. Here we found the people even more open than in Kaimana. There were more visible manifestations of the Spirit, and the pastor and leaders had an ease about them. Nabire stands out in my mind for several reasons, including the amazing meals. Twice they fed us lobster tails the size of my thigh. Even without butter, these lobsters tasted buttery. They also fed us huge local crabs and shrimp at nearly every meal.

Our last night in Nabire we prayed for a man, a former church elder, who had been paralyzed with a stroke nine years before, as well as a younger man who three years earlier had suffered a high fever for five days that left him paralyzed in his hands, arms, and feet. We prayed for two hours. Afterward, the older man got out of his chair, albeit with some difficulty, and walked with some assistance. He was lucid and no longer drooling. The younger man raised his hands and arms above his head and had full feeling in his hands and feet. At this juncture he had to use the toilet, and while his family took him to relieve himself, the church leaders pressed us to eat some dinner. It was now nearly 7:30 p.m., the service having begun at 4 p.m. While we were eating, the man returned for more prayer, but before we finished eating he left, so we were unable to pray for him further. I wonder if he might have been fully healed had we not been "servicing our stomachs." His paralysis was caused by a spirit. [We were never able to find out what happened to him afterward.]

That night, we also prayed for a thirty-year-old deaf woman. She was from a tribe whose women grow facial hair, but she was otherwise fine-featured, with bright eyes and straight, white teeth. She had been diagnosed with leukemia, but a medication mistake had caused her to lose her hearing. I have not heard of this before, so the story may have lost something in the translation. This woman received substantial healing, but she was not fully healed. Her left ear opened, but she struggled to distinguish *d's* from *r's*. However, *"puji tuhan"* (praise the Lord) was clear.

The day before we left Nabire, we received word that a church leader in Jayapura, Papua's capital, named Tobias had died. He was also a high-ranking government official many expected to be the next mayor. On our return trip to Surabaya we were scheduled to lay over in Jayapura, so we took the opportunity to visit his widow.

A wake was underway, with wailing people everywhere. Many were in despair as a prophecy had been given the previous year that Tobias would have a long life. As we considered this, 1 Corinthians 13:9–10 came to mind, which reminds us that we prophesy only in part. I shared this with Tobias' widow, and this seemed to calm her somewhat.

We passed to the great room where Tobias lay in state. As we did, a man reached out to shake my hand. Last year I prayed for a blind man who was 95 percent healed in his left eye but with no success in the right. Despite our encouragement that he return for more prayer, we did not see him again. I had often wondered what became of him. Had he been so discouraged by the lack of healing in his right eye that he did not return? Was he satisfied with the healing in just one eye? Had circumstances prevented his return? Had the Lord subsequently healed his right eye? There was no way to know.

But this was the man! As I shook his hand, I could see that both eyes were clear, and he smiled broadly as he pointed to both and then gave me a thumbs-up sign. Clearly the Lord had finished healing him! [However, with no interpreter nearby, I was unable to learn the story of how Jesus completed His work in this man's eyes, and I have not been able to find out since.]

I walked by Tobias' casket one last time. He had cotton stuffed into each nostril, perhaps a local custom. Remembering that one of Jesus' resurrections involved merely touching the coffin, I placed one hand on it and another on Tobias' stomach. He had already been dead for two days, and I could feel the coldness of his body through his suit.

I said, "Tobias, if you are going to get up, now is the time! Awake!" However, Tobias did not stir. For a moment, I was certain he had moved, but he continued lying there while the mourners beat their chests and wept. I turned and left in silence.

The thrill of victory (a blind man healed) was only two steps away from the agony of defeat (Tobias still dead). Yet we press on, always carrying around in our bodies the death of the Lord

Jesus as well as His resurrection. Death is the last enemy to be destroyed—but it will be destroyed (1 John 3:8). That victory cannot come soon enough, and I hope to see some raised from the dead before Resurrection Day. Even so, come quickly, Lord Jesus!

October 14, 2013—
Los Angeles

It was a busy weekend here in California. On Friday and Saturday, some friends from the Conejo Valley Healing Rooms sponsored a regional healing training event. On Saturday, I taught a compressed section on deliverance.

During ministry time, I prayed for a young woman who had a heartbreaking story of betrayal and loss. To keep her confidence, that is about all I can say. I will share, however, that the key to breaking open the touch she received from the Lord was a tattoo she had received in the aftermath of miscarrying her first pregnancy. Often spirits of despair, depression, death, and (at times) suicide attach themselves to such losses, and a tattoo simply binds those spirits more tightly to their host. I nearly missed this, but when I got stuck at one point, I stopped and asked the Lord, "Jesus, what am I missing?" At that moment, I felt led to ask if she had tattoos. She said she did and showed them to me, and it was then that we were able to push forward.

I know this is controversial for some. That is OK. I am writing this primarily as a training tool for those who would like to be more effective, especially in ministry to those who grieve, and particularly to those who have miscarried and/or aborted children. I also want to alert people to the hazards associated with tattoos (Lev. 19:28).

Yesterday (Sunday) I was at Foothills Christian Church in El Cajon, near San Diego. Several people were touched by the Lord, including a couple of rather visible healings of skeletal conditions, including knees and ankles. One woman was healed of deafness in about fifteen seconds, and as she hit the floor under the power of God, she yelled, "It's so loud! It's so loud! It's hurting my ears!" She had been wearing hearing aids for more than a decade. In addition, the Lord relieved many who were suffering from despair, depression, suicidal thoughts, and the like. I have received a few follow-up emails this morning from those to whom the Lord ministered.

November 21, 2013— Melbourne, Australia

Now here is a different one. Roger and I are going with a small team to a house in a suburb of Melbourne in about twenty minutes. This house has a poltergeist, which has been throwing objects around and generally creating panic. The wife/mother took the children and left yesterday, and the construction workers who've been remodeling the house ran off. The husband/father called in some psychics and others of this ilk, and they told him "to scream at it." Somehow he was given Roger's number, and so we are "going into battle" (spiritually, anyway) this morning.

We evicted the spirit. Here's what happened, in detail.

The tenant and his family had been tormented by an evil presence in their rented house since they moved in several months ago. One night, they were sitting in the living room when objects began moving around and then flew at them as they sat on the couch watching TV. They weren't sure what to think of that, so they just went to bed.

The problems continued to escalate, ranging from small objects flying at them from across the room and then a grandfather clock, up to the point of the poltergeist manifesting itself. Once, the wife was in the kitchen doing dishes at night. She looked out the window and saw the reflection of the ghost standing behind her. It wore a black trench coat and fedora and had red eyes. She turned around to face it, but it evaporated as she watched. She turned back around to finish doing the dishes, and it reappeared behind her—and that time, it touched her. That freaked her out, so she ran into the other room.

Later, she woke up to see "Daniel"—at some point the spirit told her its name—standing over her and breathing on her. That happened to her a few times and also to the couple's two boys, who would wake up in the middle of the night to see it standing menacingly in their doorway.

The family asked a Catholic exorcist to come out, but the diocese told them there was a backlog of requests for cleansings in their area and the exorcist was overworked—but he would get to them "presently."

So yesterday the homeowner called in a paranormal research team, which included some kind of pastor, to get rid of the spirit. (They arrived with ectoplasm machines and all kinds of other gear, but not the Holy Spirit.) When one of the team members crawled up a built-in ladder on the wall of the master closet into the attic, "Daniel" grabbed him by the neck and pinned him against the beam of the house, suspending him in midair. Two other team members heard his choking sounds and climbed the ladder after him. Each grabbed an ankle, pulling him free from "Daniel's" grip. The three of them all fell out of the attic onto the closet floor. Then the entire team fled the house, never to return.

This morning, when my overnight flight arrived in Melbourne, Roger greeted me at the airport with the words, "Do you want to go clear a haunted house?"

I would have preferred not to, but he had already made arrangements. So we went straight there.

"We should probably pray," he said as we parked outside.

I agreed. As we did, I started getting a vision. I pulled out a piece of paper and drew what I was seeing.

"This is the layout of the house," I said, "and these are the problem areas."

One of them was in the back right, a bedroom where we later found out the two boys slept. "There's something about the floor here," I said.

While we were in the house praying over those bedrooms, "Daniel" appeared to us. It was wearing a black or brown overcoat and a fedora, and it had glowing red eyes.

When we went into the kitchen to pray, a three-foot-tall cloud of ectoplasm formed at eye level and swirled like a small tornado, and blood began pouring out of the dining room walls into the kitchen, like something out of a horror movie. It was crazy.

We commanded the spirit to leave and heard a low, audible moan that turned into a wail as the ectoplasm began circling the ceiling of the kitchen. Then suddenly it seemed to be sucked through the wall toward the back part of the house, where most of the activity had taken place, then out of the building. Immediately, the blood stopped pouring down the walls, leaving only light stains behind.

Later, someone found an article on microfiche at the library detailing a murder that had taken place on the property many decades before. The victim's body had been buried underneath the floorboard in the children's room that I had pointed out while sketching my vision before entering the house.

I assure you what I am telling you is literally and factually correct, though some of you may question my sanity as you're reading it.

December 3, 2013—
Los Angeles

Yesterday I was invited to speak at Vanguard University (an Assembly of God school). After both the 8 a.m. and 9 a.m. Old Testament classes, we had a short ministry time.

In the first class, a girl's foot was partially healed; she said she could feel her tendon "popping" back into place as the Holy Spirit moved over her. I think it is safe to say that many of the students were shocked to see this happen before their eyes. I wish it had been a total healing, but certain factors were militating against that ministry time. We also prayed for several other students after class dismissed, including a girl who had been in a car accident some weeks before. Her whiplash, damaged spine, and shoulders had not yet recovered, nor had they stopped hurting. However, the Lord healed her, and she left the classroom rejoicing.

In the second class, the spirit of prophecy began moving with several specific words for the students. One woman received a word about gifts of counseling and an ability to untangle twisted internal lives. It further seemed that she had been considering a career in counseling and that she had a particular interest in children with autism or Down syndrome. She began crying as it was revealed that many people had come against her for her unique personality and unusual behaviors. She later shared that she had, in fact, been torn between a career as a counseling pastor or a high school counselor. She also stated why she had a particular soft spot for autistic children, saying, "I rarely share this in public, but since all of this was revealed by God, I will share it here: I have Asperger's syndrome." It was holy and awe-inspiring that the Lord would speak so profoundly and specifically to this woman.

Another word, which I especially liked, was directed toward a young man who seemed to have a gift for preaching. The man responded to the Word, saying he had been called to preach at age six. Then the Holy Spirit fell on him with increasing waves of power, including giving several other specific pieces of information about his life.

A young woman of about twenty said she'd had lifelong problems with fear, anxiety, claustrophobia, depression, and upset stomach. She had allergies to wheat, gluten, dark fruit, citrus, milk, and two other kinds of food I can't remember now. She'd also had her gallbladder removed surgically, but the intended benefit never materialized, and she was now intolerant of fat. As she spoke, I kept thinking, "This must be Freemasonry. It has all the hallmarks." Just as I was about to ask her, she said, "My grandfather was a very high-ranking Freemason, as was my father." Well, that sealed the deal.

[When someone joins a Freemasonic order, they pledge themselves and their seed forever (into perpetuity) to the service of Jahbulon (a demonic spirit that inhabits a made-up personality that is a combination of God, Baal, and the Egyptian god of war). Jahbulon takes this vow seriously, even if the people do not—and when someone in the family line departs from Freemasonry, they tend to be struck with mental illness or other diseases. For a more detailed discussion of Freemasonry and the signs that spirits associated with it are operating in a person's life, see Appendix B.]

I asked the girl to come to the side of the room where we could pray semiprivately (class had dismissed by then). I led her in a prayer of repentance for her forefathers' sin, renouncing the lodge and its benefits and curses, and Jahbulon. After these opening prayers, I commanded Jahbulon to "come out!" She began coughing and burping, apologizing profusely for being so rude. "But I can't help it!" she protested sheepishly. I told her it was OK at that moment; it is common when people get free. I then spoke to each of the food allergies by turn, commanding them to "come out!" She coughed and burped as each came out.

When it was all done, her face was glowing, and she said, "My stomach always hurts. It's like there's a brick in it. In fact, my back always hurts because I hunch over to compensate for the stomach pain. For the first time in I don't know how long, neither my stomach nor my back hurts! It also feels like I have a hole in my throat and my chest, but it is a good hole—like something dark and heavy and oppressive is missing. What happened just now?" I explained to her the dangers of the Masonic lodge, and I told her she was experiencing the freedom Jesus offers.

I told her to try eating small quantities of the food to which she had been allergic. I am waiting on a report from her or her professor, but based on previous ministry sessions of this type, I know what I expect the answer to be: no more food allergies. [The professor later confirmed that she was fine.]

Honestly, I don't know what is going on with deliverance these days, but it seems to be off the charts with demons of many types coming out—often very strong ones that have been entrenched for years. I certainly haven't been trying to provoke anything, but all I can say is, "Watch out! The deliverance tsunami is surging!" Bring it on, Jesus! We've been waiting for You to do this for a long, long time.

December 17, 2013— Los Angeles

My ministry trip to Dallas continued through Sunday morning, when I preached at the Frisco Vineyard. The sermon went well, and the ministry time was very rich. Two healings particularly stand out in my mind. The first was a woman with a long, complex history of pain in her bladder and lower abdomen. She also had massive pain in her back and legs, which had been diagnosed as sciatica and fibromyalgia. This woman had been a leader in the Rainbow for Girls youth organization within the Freemasons. Both parents had belonged to the Freemasons, as had her grandfather. Once we dealt with the Freemasonry, healing came over her body. She wasn't healed instantaneously, but after about twenty minutes she began weeping, then rejoicing, as the Lord touched her. All the pain left her body. On her way out of the building, she remarked to someone, "No more visits to the doctor for me!"

The second person was a boy (approximately ten or twelve years old) who had a problem in his sacrum, IBS, and stunted growth due to its attendant nutritional deficiencies. When his parents brought him for prayer, I asked them what has almost become the Diagnostics 101 question these days: "Do you have any Freemasonry in your family background?" It turned out the father's father and the mother's grandfather had been Freemasons. If you haven't guessed it by now, Freemasonry is *far more common* and *far more serious* than most people realize. I started to pray for the boy, but then I stopped, sensing more was needed. I asked his parents to join me in praying, whereupon the father said they had three other sons. Should they join us as well? I said yes, then all seven of us went through the prayer time together.

Immediately, the first boy began crying and tried to hide his face. I encouraged him not to feel ashamed of his tears, explaining that sometimes when Jesus touches us, we are overwhelmed with joy, wonder, or thankfulness. Something was clearly happening, and the boy soon indicated his stomach was no longer hurting. His mother began sobbing, as this had been a lifelong battle. So I put my arm around her and said, as Jesus told us to do, "The kingdom of heaven has come nigh unto you." She cried even harder.

Today I got the following report from the pastor: "OK, dude, [the little boy] is completely healed. He had a complete GI and colon check today. I don't know how much of the story you know, but man, this is awesome. Thank You, Lord." [For the record, I have not altered that message at all, except to remove the individual's name.]

All over the world, the kingdom of heaven is forcefully advancing, and forceful men and women seize it. It's time that we all join in, don't you think?

PILLAR 4

Presence

*And the servant of the Lord must not strive; but
be gentle unto all men, apt to teach, patient.*
—2 Timothy 2:24, kjv

STRIVING IS A term that is essentially obsolete in the Christian lexicon, but in a former generation, believers were urged not to strive—meaning not to work with fleshly energy to seek favor from God or to achieve certain spiritual outcomes. One dictionary defines this sense of the term as "to exert oneself vigorously; try hard."[1]

In the passage I've cited, however, striving has a different sense. The Greek word means to engage in a war of words, quarreling, wrangling. It can also mean to bring a lawsuit. In addition, it connotes the energy expended when men engage in hand-to-hand combat (i.e., fight to the death). The opposite of striving is gentleness and patience along with an ability to instruct others, presumably to a higher life.

This admonition against striving, so often overlooked in our day, is specifically directed at "servants of the Lord." It is noteworthy that Paul wrote this to Timothy, his spiritual son. The immediate context (2 Tim. 2:22–26) suggests that in the midst of controversies, especially about speculative matters, Timothy (and others) might be tempted to become harsh, dogmatic, doctrinaire, or "hard line." In contradistinction to this, Paul urges Timothy to "hold the line" without becoming "hard line." It is a subtle but important distinction.

We live in a time when it has become acceptable to stir up controversies. Much of news reporting, talk show radio, and blogging is done in such a way that people will become agitated and indignant about wrongs committed, whether real or perceived. Often that indignation boils over without anyone bothering to check the facts. John Wimber used to call this tabloid journalism, in which all sense of dispassionate assessment has been discarded. Even the practice of posting comments under online news articles is focused around stirring things up, nowadays known as "engagement." The things being stirred are the grievances the publishers want people to think they have suffered.

In contrast to the fleshly, arrogant, striving, tabloid behavior of our era, Christians are called to be fair-minded, temperate, and peaceable. "So then, as we have opportunity, let us do good to everyone, and especially to those who are of the household of faith" (Gal. 6:10).

A hallmark of genuine Christianity is a firm refusal to be drawn into internecine battle. This involves choosing not to revile when reviled, declining to threaten when suffering, and entrusting ourselves to Him who judges justly (1 Pet. 2:23). This is the essence of turning the other cheek. Think about it this way the next time you are tempted to strive: the enemy of your soul would love to steal your peace, your confidence, and your testimony. It may be that the very situation, word, or person tempting you to strive is in fact the very situation, word, or affront God is calling you to overcome. Tests rarely have the word "test" written all over them. So the best policy is to live this way continuously. Here is the striving we *do* want: "Strive for peace with everyone, and for the holiness without which no one will see the LORD" (Heb. 12:14).

January 23, 2014— Champaign, Illinois

It was 0 degrees Fahrenheit (around -18 degrees Celsius) this morning with twenty-five mile-per-hour winds, but inside the Champaign Vineyard Church, it was red-hot. Seven hundred hungry people gathered to worship God and hear Randy Clark and Robby Dawkins preach. Last night, US National Vineyard Director Philip Strout opened the meeting with a simple prayer of "Come again, Holy Spirit!" This morning, the Holy Spirit began falling before the sermon was done, and there wasn't a dry eye in the room.

Here are two takeaways from this morning to chew on:

1. God is looking for hungry people who will press in and not give up.

2. When your desperation exceeds your concern over what people think of you, breakthrough occurs.

Have you stopped pressing in? Has a need for respectability in the eyes of your family, your peers, or your church stopped you from doing whatever it takes to connect with God? If you answered yes to either question, it is time to pray again, "Come, Holy Spirit!"

Randy, a former Southern Baptist minister, told in his sermon how he was driven to desperation. Church was killing him. Ministry was killing him. The disillusionment of Christians who didn't love the Bible or each other was killing his wife. Their marriage was falling apart, and she begged him to leave the ministry to teach school.

Then God got hold of him at a John Wimber meeting in Dallas. Beloved, pray to get hungry (Matt. 5:6)!

Nobody wants their life ruined. We do our best to do right,

but sometimes our best isn't enough. When we come to the end of ourselves, that is when mercy and grace intercept us. If you are at the end of yourself, this is the time for mercy. It is the season of visitation. He is come.

February 8, 2014—
Cancún, Quintana Roo, Mexico

The meetings here have begun exceptionally well. The first night the team ministered about sixty kilometers south of Cancún, at La Iglesia Nuevo Punto de Vida (New Point of Life Church) in Playa del Carmen. It was standing room only. Two disabled people were healed, five people with frozen shoulders received their mobility and lost their pain, seven people with long-term sinus and asthma conditions were healed, and several other healings occurred, including a pregnant woman with a hernia the size of a fist, which simply closed and vanished. She unashamedly grabbed my hand and put it on her stomach to show me where the hole had been and now was no longer.

In addition to all the healings, the level of impartation was eye-popping, and the word of prophecy was moving with great accuracy. Many people simply crumpled to the floor under the power of God as the Lord revealed their dreams and prayers prophetically.

February 10, 2014—
Los Angeles

I arrived at LAX from southern Mexico last night at 11:57 p.m. As I have already reported, it was quite a trip. During the latter part of the conference, so many healings and deliverances occurred that I lost track of them all, and I'm sure the team did as well. We also had many salvations as those who formerly thought they were Christian realized that if *this* is the Christian life, they were lacking something (Jesus Himself).

Here are a few samples of the things that happened over the last three days: One woman with a paralyzed leg and foot received sensation back in that limb along with the ability to walk normally. Another man testified that his diabetic neuropathy had vanished and that he had slept through the night for the first time in two years. Another woman had a hard, marblelike cyst in her wrist that protruded prominently under her skin; the cyst vanished while she received prayer, and she also received full use of her wrist back. Jesus performed many other healings, including six healings of frozen shoulders. The six frozen shoulders were healed in front of the room when I had all of them line up for prayer. To detail all the healings would be a book in itself if they were written. When this kind of abundant miracle outpouring is happening, it is easy to understand what John wrote when he said if they were all written the world itself couldn't contain the books (John 21:25).

One other thing happened at that meeting that's worth telling in great detail.

One woman had, as a child, been dedicated to Satan and a local deity. The dedication ritual included a man being killed and then dismembered before her eyes, and she was repeatedly covered in his blood. While we were holding a meeting at a church called Mundo de Fe, a woman started manifesting a demon right in the middle of the crowd. Sometime before that conference began, she had been kicked out of the church because she kept interrupting worship and the leaders didn't know what to do with her. I asked a team to take her into a side room so I could keep teaching. During a break, I went into the room to check on them.

The team—which now numbered eight people—was stuck on the woman's deliverance. When I walked in, she was lying flat on her back on the floor. She looked at me and said, "We don't like you," and she instantly began to levitate off the floor until she was at eye level with me.

The guy leading the prayer time said, "This is what we ran into. We're stuck."

I looked at the levitating woman and said, "Who are you?"

"Apollyon," the spirit answered.

Apollyon is mentioned in Revelation 9:11 as the gatekeeper of hell and presumably its second-in-command. I remember thinking, "I wish a Christian were here to deal with this. Where is John Wimber when I need him?"

Suddenly, what David said to Goliath came into my mind: "I've killed the lion and the bear, and I will kill you, too, you uncircumcised Philistine!" (See 1 Samuel 17:36.)

A surge of faith rooted in the memory of past victories over evil spirits suddenly hit me. I remembered all the other powerful spirits I'd seen vanquished and thought, "What is the number two demon in hell compared to the power of Jesus?"

With that, I said, "You come out in the name of Jesus!" The spirit screamed—and came out. The levitating woman crashed to the floor.

She was totally free.

The team members were all excited with their various experiences of healing, deliverance, inner healing, impartation, and more. Most said they had only heard and never seen things like what they witnessed during our time in southern Mexico. God truly is not a theory!

I sense that these meetings in Cancún were much more than just another conference. Mesoamerica is ripe for a sweeping move of God for many reasons. It is still struggling with the aftermath of wars in Guatemala, El Salvador, and Nicaragua that ended thirty years ago. Additionally, the impact of rising violence from the Mexican drug cartels cannot be overestimated. Moreover, when the local Mayan people were converted to Catholicism, they were never truly evangelized. There is a strange mix of native Mayan religion underneath the outward veneer of Christianity (both Catholic and Protestant). In this environment, proclaiming the kingdom of God levels the playing field, bringing salvation to the lost, healing to the sick, driving out demons, and setting the captives free. The local leaders have asked me to return to work with them. They have a vision for a regional outpouring of the Spirit that would encompass southern Mexico as well as Belize, Guatemala, Honduras, El Salvador, Costa Rica, Nicaragua, and Panama. I expect the Lord will open a wide door of favor and ministry among the nations and the peoples of Central America, as He has done these last four years in Australia. This would partially fulfill a prophetic word I received nearly three years ago from a man who formerly traveled with Francis MacNutt as his "staff prophet."

[Francis MacNutt was a Harvard-educated Roman Catholic priest who was influential in the Catholic Charismatic Renewal and who wrote several books, including *Healing*, *The Power to Heal*, and *Deliverance From Evil Spirits*. We became friends toward the end of his life, and I continue to hold events alongside his widow, Judith.]

On a personal note, there is always a certain kind of "come down" in the aftermath of these trips. Mine is particularly acute at present because I am returning to pack up our belongings and move. John Wimber used to joke that he would come home from ministry trips only to hear his wife say, "OK, now take out the trash." So it is back to the nuts and bolts of life for the next few days. However, next week a few team members will be traveling with me to a church in Washington, DC, where Jesus appeared to the crowd last June and where hundreds were healed in minutes. As I pack boxes, I'm wondering, "What will next week hold?" *¡Dios te bendiga! ¡Gloria a Dios!*

February 24, 2014—
Los Angeles

For those who question why we need deliverance ministry, the answer is simple. John 8:36 says, "So if the Son sets you free, you will be free indeed." Jesus paid for our freedom with His life, yet many believers remain bound with sin, old wounds, and demonic infestation. Some have misinterpreted this passage to read that if you are born again, you are free from all bondages and demonic influence. The reality is more nuanced than this. Jesus paid for freedom, but many have not accessed or stepped into the freedom He purchased. It is through prophetic ministry, inner healing, and deliverance that the freedom that was bought for us is released into a believer's life.

I spoke at a training event this weekend in San Diego where many, many people were freed from food allergies, lingering symptoms of multiple sclerosis, paralysis, deafness (to name only a few physical conditions), and assorted nonphysical conditions, including rape trauma, sexual bondage, and various neuroses. Several people also told me of healings they received the last time I visited that church, including someone who was healed of partial paralysis due to a crushed spine.

Upon leaving San Diego, I went to Washington, DC. The first meeting was on Thursday night at a private home. Nearly half the people present held senior management positions with the World Bank. Our hosts were eager for each of the people present to receive ministry, and the Holy Spirit graciously met their faith. Every person in the room received prophetic words, which were later confirmed as having been extremely accurate, and some also received healing and/or deliverance. The logistics of praying for even that small of a group meant that by the time we finished, the meeting had lasted five and a half hours, ending at 12:30 a.m. Said another way, praying for just five minutes with each person would have meant an hour and a half of ministry, but more in-depth ministry necessitated a longer meeting. In the end, we spent about ten to fifteen minutes with each person, although one little girl with a terrible skin condition received more in-depth prayer.

I arrived in DC tired from three busy weeks of packing and moving our household belongings to storage, feeling insufficiently prepared for these meetings. Despite this, the Lord gave me grace in speaking; several times I was conscious of His anointing. The ministry times were exceptional. Having an experienced prayer team with me was an enormous advantage. Among the healings the team verified was a tumor the size of an orange that simply vanished from a woman who also appears to have been healed of multiple sclerosis (although this latter condition requires additional medical testing for confirmation). There was also a woman afflicted with lupus who could barely walk, even with her walker. After prayer, she freely and easily walked, to the thunderous applause of the congregation. An important factor in her healing was the expulsion of a spirit of death. As it manifested, her face and lips turned ashen. Immediately upon its leaving (and I do mean immediately), normal color returned to her face and lips and she got up and walked.

There was also an assortment of about twenty paralyzed or impaired elbows, ankles, and knees that were healed in one fell swoop. One man was healed of fibromyalgia; he lay on the floor for some time weeping at his freedom from pain, while another man testified of being healed of sciatica as I was teaching, without anyone touching him. There was a man with a history of mental illness who was delivered from some very powerful demons, and when they left, he looked at me and said, "I...I...I can't believe it. My mind is clear for the first time in decades! What just happened? I feel different. It's all...*gone!*" Then he broke down, weeping. To be clear, I don't think all mental illness is demonic, but his illness clearly had a demonic component, and the Lord delivered him.

Another man was delivered from spirits associated with his past drug use and immoral lifestyle; he left a physical "deposit" of vomit on the ground as a testimony to the depth of the freedom he received, which is pretty normal. [Typically, real deliverance involves something that you can see, smell, or otherwise sense. I've heard a lot about "quiet deliverance" in which people say words but nothing really happens. In general, I don't think those instances get to the root of the issue, and those demons are still hanging around.] There was also a woman who was freed from an incubus spirit that had tormented her for several years.

And then there was a woman with dissociative identity disorder (DID), which arose from satanic ritual abuse (SRA), whom I had met on an earlier trip to the East Coast. Some DID arises from trauma other than SRA, but nearly all SRA gives rise to DID. She flew to Washington, and some of the team and I met with her prior to and throughout the conference. Due to the significant fracturing of her psyche, she would spontaneously switch between personalities, unable to hold to one. Both DID and SRA are complex, serious conditions, and rarely is either healed all at once. Nevertheless, they *can* be healed, and by the time we parted company on Sunday afternoon, she had enough stability in her personality to successfully hold the center, no longer switching between parts and alters. She is well on her way to integration!

[Over the following years, I continued meeting with her periodically as I traveled, and we were able to bring her further along. We got her down to seventeen personalities, which was a big improvement over the nearly five hundred she had when we first began. I could tell that a lot of her alternate personalities (alters) had evil spirits, and she needed to be delivered too; during one session we filled half of a thirty-three-gallon trash bag with vomit as they came out. She later made some personal decisions that stopped her healing progress—so while I have seen many people get fully integrated, so far she has not.]

Deliverance is not integration, but if you're going to minister to DID, you have to be able to do both. (The alter personalities may need deliverance too.) Occasionally, an alter doesn't need deliverance, but typically they all do because the demons are attached to the trauma. If the personalities don't need deliverance, they still need inner healing.

The highest number of personalities I've ever heard of was a woman with more than forty thousand. It took the person working with her about five and a half years to deal with all that. The first DID victim John Wimber ever had my wife and me work on was at the Vineyard in Anaheim—a woman who had 4,700 some-odd personalities. We and one of the staff pastors met with her every Sunday before church because people with DID need consistency in order to make progress. After nine months she was totally integrated and healed. Since then I've found some methods that work better, so the process has sped up. It might take a few weeks or months of regular meetings for most cases at this time. For whatever reason, people with DID seem to sense who is safe, and they seek out such people to pray for them.

How can we summarize all of this? First, the kingdom of heaven is at hand. This was Jesus' proclamation (Mark 1:14–15), and it is also to be ours (Matt. 10:7). I don't know why these particular words are important, but I have seen with my own eyes that proclaiming this message has a dynamic and catalytic effect. Second, when we announce the gospel of the kingdom, the Lord will work with us to confirm the message (Mark 16:20). He delights to confirm His Word!

February 28, 2014—
Los Angeles

It's been an interesting mixed bag of ministry encounters this week. On Monday I was in Long Beach teaching a class on ministry skills. On Wednesday I was in Lomita teaching on power gifts. Last night I spoke at a Redondo Beach home group, teaching on distance healing and its relationship to miracles. In each of these places, I tried to coach the prayer teams that gathered around each person who requested prayer, rather than ministering myself. The Holy Spirit moved in each meeting, but the intensity was uneven. I have been thinking about this phenomenon: Those who are seeing more manifest power (however that is displayed) typically have a faith level that causes them to contend for the release. This is especially important when things don't "just happen" at the moment the prayer begins.

[A note on distance healing: I've seen large numbers of people healed from a distance. I held one meeting in China in which people brought cloths and towels, and we prayed over them. We heard later that several hundred people nationwide had been healed from those cloths. For many people, this is a stretch. You may not have seen it, but Acts tells us Paul did it. Jesus did it with the centurion's servant and the Syrophoenician woman's daughter—and He said what He did, we would do in even greater measure. So this should just be part of the normal Christian life. However, it's not intercessory prayer. We're not just asking God to heal someone and bless them. We are speaking a word as Jesus did, and the word releases something. When this is happening, it's not a decree or proclamation. This is the gift of faith in operation, and when that is present, God does what we say, even if the person we are praying for is thousands of miles away. Faith calls things that are not as though they were.]

Scripture says one of the fruits of the Spirit is faithfulness

(Gal. 5:22). Commonly, we interpret *faithful* to mean "reliable" in the sense that we show up for work on time, pay our bills, are loyal to those who logically should expect our loyalty, and so on, and these are all good. However, the fruit of faithfulness could just as well refer to being "stalwart" or "doughty." Considered this way, it may be that faithfulness is a necessary trigger for gifts of healing, miracles, or prophecy. Perhaps we could even say that the gifts require the fruit to be fully activated; without them, the fruit of the Spirit can simply become a metaphor for "being nice." I'm all for being nice, but I think life in the Spirit has many more dimensions than this.

On the subject of distance healing, I had a Skype appointment with a woman yesterday. I generally dislike praying for people over Skype for a variety of reasons. However, in this instance I was willing to do it. She was delivered of spirits of Freemasonry, but she was also delivered of generational spirits of false doctrine. The backstory is that her grandfather had been a Unitarian and had led nearly his entire family into this heresy. I don't think we take false teaching and false doctrine seriously enough when praying for those who are afflicted with long-term conditions.

March 18, 2014— Geraldton, Western Australia

The first night of meetings went well; attendance was good, especially for a Monday night. As I often do when first visiting a city or congregation, I taught on the kingdom of God. The crowd was responsive, and several people appear to have been healed of different conditions. One woman had recently injured her right wrist. Another was a medical doctor with a long-term stomach/upper GI problem. I am awaiting confirmation of his healing.

As the meeting was wrapping up, some people lingered for additional prayer. They received deep touches from the Lord, including a woman who was delivered from some powerful ancestral Aboriginal spirits. Her deliverance included not just coughing but coughing up something from deep within her body. The "ejecta" coming from her mouth was first blood but then turned into something gray/black with a distinct and unusual texture and odor. She was a happy camper afterward, and it resulted in her receiving healing from several conditions. The kingdom of God has come to Geraldton too! As they say, "Just another day at the office."

March 20, 2014— Los Angeles

I have been working with sexually broken people—heterosexual, homosexual, lesbian, bisexual, transgendered, bestial, and more—since the 1980s when I was working for John Wimber at Vineyard Anaheim. It started with prison ministry among the HIV-positive men at the Del Norte unit of the Chino Men's prison (70 percent of the inmates were gay, cross-dressers, or transgendered). Since then, I have seen literally hundreds of LGBTQ people have their sexuality redeemed. If you include the heterosexually broken, the number climbs into the thousands. Change is possible, and it is far more common than many suppose.

During his earthly ministry, Jesus confronted some religious leaders at one point, saying, "You are in error because you do not know the Scriptures or the power of God" (Matt. 22:29, NIV). In our day, many Christian leaders have gone soft on the unambiguous witness of Scripture about *any* kind of sexual activity outside the confines of monogamous heterosexual marriage. Sexual brokenness is a much bigger issue than just the LGBTQ aspect of it. The vast majority of American society suffers from some form of it. Matthew 22:29 reminds us that healing and restoration on this issue strongly depend on whether we hold fast to the teachings of Scripture as infallible and as the rule of all faith and practice.

Jesus also said there was a second part of the problem: not knowing God's power. The Holy Spirit is not an "it." He is not merely a divine, external influence for good. He is the third Person of the Godhead, come to reside in us. He is far more committed to our sanctification and transformation than we are. In our day, many speak of the power of God, but few expect His power to intersect us at the deepest level of our human fallenness. Or perhaps we do not wish to meet Him there. Yet the power of God is profound enough—His mercy great enough—even to redeem broken sexuality now in this life. Sexual redemption only comes through the manifest power of God.

For too long, the only two choices the world has been given are a) accept sexual brokenness because it cannot be changed, or b) persecute those who are broken (whether by seeking to stone a woman caught in adultery or by hating those who are LGBTQ). Is it any wonder they choose the first option? It is time for the church to offer a third way: Jesus offers freedom from sexual brokenness.

The sexually broken people I have worked with longed for freedom. I have seen their tears of anguish before and tears of joy after they have been set free. I see these things while meeting with them in private. In public, most have been wearing the facade of being "out and proud."

I know many will disagree strongly with what I have written, and I anticipate a sharp response. I can only tell what I have seen: thousands redeemed from fallen sexuality through the active, dynamic power of God. Paul saw this as well. He wrote to the Corinthian church about sexual immorality in general and homosexuality in particular, saying, "And such were some of you. But you were washed, you were sanctified, you were justified in the name of the Lord Jesus Christ and by the Spirit of our God" (1 Cor. 6:11). The kingdom of God is a message of hope.

Could it be said that we err in our day because we do not know the Scripture or the power of God? Instead, may we say with Paul, "I am not ashamed of the gospel, for it is the power of God for salvation [and transformation] to everyone who believes" (Rom. 1:16).

March 25, 2014—
Perth, Western Australia

Last night's meeting was held in a packed house. I spoke about the life of John the Baptist as a gauge of where things stand in the Lord's timing for the western part of the country. The ministry time saw many people touched powerfully, including some who were knocked to the floor by the Holy Spirit. One young woman received a prophetic word, which confirmed much of what she had already seen God doing in her life. She was overwhelmed by how God spoke to her so personally and accurately.

There was also a woman present who was suffering with multiple sclerosis (MS). We prayed for her, and after a bit her numbness and paralysis lifted. We walked her around to test everything out before concluding the prayer time. This MS was related to physical trauma (she had been beaten in the past) as well as our old nemesis Freemasonry. She appears to have been healed, but as with all such things, we await medical confirmation.

We also prayed for a woman with macular degeneration. The Lord closed a hole in her field of vision the size of a US quarter and removed nearly all the visual "floaters." The blindness was related to ancestral Buddhist spirits (she was a first-generation Chinese believer). There was also a man with a horseshoe kidney who was in extreme pain. We couldn't even touch his abdomen due to the pain. After about twenty minutes of prayer and extreme heat (like a toaster browning bread—he could feel it, as did we), he was pressing on his body, stating that the pain was dramatically better, at a tolerable level. However, his body was still burning when we left, and I suspect he was completely healed overnight. [On a subsequent trip, we learned he had been.]

March 31, 2014—
Perth

Yesterday I finished up the SEERS Conference at Living Faith Community Church here in Perth. The level of ministry built steadily through the ten sessions, and last night, just as I was closing the message, a heavy wave of the Holy Spirit hit the room. It reminded me of the moves of God we saw in 2011, including the fiery manifestations that were sent to Australia from southeastern Europe. Many had never seen or experienced anything like this, especially the fourteen- to thirty-year-olds, but they loved it! Although the conference was about the seer's gift, plenty of healing and deliverance was going on too.

One Frenchman who didn't believe in Jesus came forward for prayer for his family relationships to be healed, particularly with his wife and daughter. I am always amazed by how the common struggles of the human condition unite us. Everyone wants to have happy, healthy family relationships, yet so many do not, and it is a source of deep grief and disappointment. This becomes an opportunity for meaningful conversations about the Lord. I talked with the Frenchman about the principles of the kingdom and how following them will lead to more successful relationships. He agreed that made sense. As we prayed, something broke, and he said he hadn't ever experienced anything like this before. Then in amazement he exclaimed, "I'm crying like a baby!" When I realized his wife was standing close by, I prayed with her and then with the two of them. The kingdom of God is breaking out all over Western Australia on this trip.

Last night I was in Rockingham. The Holy Spirit *erupted* during worship, and many people fell into prophetic ecstasy, laughter, and more. One woman said she could see angels present, then she fell into a trance. Another man was taken up in a vision to heaven. This man fell face down on the floor and was out for about forty-five minutes. His body was there, but whether he was in it or out of it wasn't immediately clear. When he rejoined us, he reported a tremendous word that was akin to Ezekiel's vision of dry bones. It was clear this wasn't a made-up experience as the Holy Spirit proceeded to crash in on people yet again in confirmation. I haven't seen a prophetic gathering of this type in a long while, but if this is where things are headed, Western Australia is definitely up for a ride.

April 9, 2014—
Waiake, Auckland, New Zealand

Tonight things get underway in earnest. New Zealand has a history of great spiritual dynamism (note the name of the country—"Zeal"), and while pockets of fervor remain, in other areas things have died down since the spiritual renewal that took place between the 1950s and 1980s. I have a sense of expectancy. There is something more elemental, raw, and earthy (in all the right ways) in the spiritual climate here than I have experienced even in Australia. I am praying the Lord stirs up this nation as in times past. It is a smaller country (one-sixth Australia's population), so awakening should spread even more readily here than there.

The first day, one of our hosts took us to an overlook. As we were walking up, I asked if it was a caldera. She replied that most of the peaks in this country are volcanoes, so yes it was.

"Then there must be a spirit that lives up here," I replied. Somewhat surprised, she asked how I knew that. "That's just the way it works," I answered.

Sure enough, we found that the caldera, formerly a children's playground, was cordoned off and marked as a "sacred site." On its rim stood a grove of small trees where the local spirit lived. The *iwi* (native councils) have been aggressively reclaiming once-sacred sites and repudiating the Christianity the British brought two hundred years ago. So we may see some rather dramatic power encounters on this trip.

And in fact we did. As we neared the trees while walking the perimeter of the caldera, I said, "There's a spirit over there in those trees." Our host said, "How do you know that? I don't feel anything." (Which was surprising to me because she is very prophetic.) But as we rounded the edge of the caldera, I looked into the trees, and sitting in the crotch of one of them was a spirit.

I pointed it out to our host. "Don't you see that spirit over there?"

She said no. I said, "It's got leathery brown skin and bulging eyes, and it's wearing something made out of jagged teeth, some kind of waistband to cover the genitalia."

It was kind of hunched up, like Gollum from *The Lord of the Rings*. She still couldn't see anything. So I told that spirit it couldn't stay up there and needed to leave. It ejected from the tree and over the side of the caldera and was gone. I didn't see any more spirits up there.

I realize this isn't something most people experience. So let me offer some explanation.

Calderas are high places, and people who are into New Age or witchcraft really like those. We see this all over the Old Testament, and it has not changed one iota in the modern period. Therefore, if you go hiking you might see little piles of rocks, cairns, or evidence of people having poured out a drink offering or sacrificing an animal. I've also seen such things on the tops of buildings in cities. In Hawaii, they call them *heiaus*. That's where they summon the spirits. [One of the ways Hawaiians summon spirits is by dancing the hula. New Zealanders do something similar, but the dance has a different name.] If I happen to be hiking, I'm always on the lookout because I assume there are probably some around.

Typically, if you evict a spirit over a high place, it will impact the region. Then there will be a greater openness to the gospel, more healings. We had a situation like that in Costa Rica, on a peak called Poás; this was also the name of the spirit that lived up there. When we got rid of him, it triggered an explosion in the volcano, and that set off a chain of eruptions in a string of volcanoes throughout Central America, in sequence, all the way into the northern tier of South America. After that, there was a greater release of evangelism, and many people came to the Lord.

There were also many healings, including a little boy with a club that was turned completely around and facing backward; his bones straightened out, and the foot rotated to point in the right direction. His father came to me and grasped my feet, thanking me for healing his son. I told him the Lord had done it, and it wasn't me, so to please get off the floor because it was embarrassing.

June 2, 2014—
Adelaide, South Australia

Saturday started with a trip to the Psychic Expo. I went to this expo with a church with which I worked in order to engage in evangelism among the attendees. People who attend such exhibitions are generally quite open to the supernatural, so they readily accept prophetic words, healing, and other supernatural activity when included as part of the evangelistic effort. We still share the message of Jesus and the truths of Scripture; we just also include these supernatural demonstrations of the gospel when sharing. For reasons unexplained (other than the prayers of the local Christian population, which has been praying for it to go away), the number of exhibitors was down about 75 percent this year(!), as was attendance. Notwithstanding, we had some great healings in our booth.

At one point, a woman walked up with two younger girls. She asked for prayer for depression. As we began praying, a word of knowledge came forth, asking what had happened when she was sixteen. She pointed at one of the girls and said, "I got pregnant with her!" It turned out she was a Christian of sorts, albeit not particularly consecrated (Why else would she be attending a psychic expo?). Nevertheless, she understood the basics of Christianity, so we asked if she understood that while her daughter was a blessing to her, the manner in which she had been conceived (i.e., out of wedlock) wasn't God's best. She acknowledged that was true, so we administered the forgiveness of Christ to that time when she was sixteen. She broke and started weeping. We prayed about the fear and shame of being pregnant and still in high school. She fell under the power of God as more tears flowed.

Suddenly, she sat bolt upright and said, "It's gone!" *Huh? What's gone?* "The depression! Just now it left like that! Wow! This is incredible!" Her face glowed, and she was quite animated.

About that time, the woman's daughter stepped into the booth, and within a few moments the team had led her to Christ, and she was baptized in the Holy Spirit. She was speaking in tongues and vibrating quite perceptibly. I went over to the other girl. She eyed me dubiously as she looked at her two friends. "Yes?" she asked.

"I was just wondering if you have had any contact with spirits," I said. "Maybe this was in a séance or a table-tipping exercise, something like that."

"Well, my friends are into that kind of thing, but I haven't participated...yet," she said. "They have been trying to get me involved. I used to be really freaked out by it, but I'm getting more comfortable with it. There is a spirit that comes into my bedroom, though. Her name is 'Mary.' I can't sleep when she is there."

I asked if we could pray with her about that, and she said yes. She sat down in a chair, and as we prayed for the fear to leave, she stated that she felt much better and that a heaviness had lifted from her chest. Then another word of knowledge came forth about a young man, fifteen years of age, who was hanging around her. Perhaps there was a relationship between her and this young man, or maybe he was merely interested in her. She put her hands to her cheeks and said, "Oh my gosh! How do you people know this? Yes!"

"You need to be careful of him. He isn't safe."

"Oh my gosh! Thank you! This is what I needed to hear! I really needed to hear this! How did you know? Thank you! I so needed to hear this! Thank you! Oh my gosh!"

At that point, the door was open to tell her that Jesus loved her enough to reveal such information about her and to speak to her. She was now ready to hear and receive the gospel, and so she did. This is how an *oikos* (Greek for "household," but we would say "social network") is invaded by the kingdom of God.

Later that day, a woman came into the booth for prayer. She didn't really know what she wanted, but she was at the Expo, so why not have a try? As we prayed for her, the Lord pointed out her heart and lungs. It turned out she suffered from angina, and after we commanded it to leave, she said, "What just happened? All the pain in my chest just left! That feels a lot better!"

She jumped up, walked around, and encouraged her friend to try it as well. While her friend was receiving prayer, we talked about her heart some more; she was overjoyed by how much better she felt, and she kept thanking us for praying for her. She asked if this truly meant she was healed, and we told her to ask her doctor, as we had no way of evaluating her heart there at the

Expo. Suddenly, she said, "If this Jesus can heal my heart like this, can He heal my partially blind left eye?"

With that, we prayed for her eye. For reasons unexplained, the eye was not healed, and she seemed disappointed, as were we. However, she asked for materials about the church and said she would come for further prayer, as she was certain that this Jesus who healed her heart could and would also heal her eye. We asked if she would like to receive Christ, but she wanted some time to think about that. So we gave her a Gospel of John, exchanged information, and will follow up with her later.

From the Expo I went to a Baptist church in the hills above Adelaide. On Sunday, I spoke at two churches. The second church begins its Sunday service at 3 p.m. and typically ends it at 6 p.m. We finally left the building at 9 p.m., I'm sure much to the janitor's relief.

During that six-hour period, nearly the entire congregation received prayer. I'm not particularly good at estimating crowds, but I suspect the team and I prayed for about three hundred people. Several who could barely walk were healed of ankle, knee, and back conditions. There seemed to be an anointing for scoliosis as well, and quite a few who came forward with this condition straightened up while reporting that their pains had left. One of our team members is a back specialist; she examined some of the scoliosis patients on the spot, declaring she could find no evidence of the condition (although to be absolutely sure they were healed, they would need radiographs of some type). Some also had metal in their bodies (knees, legs, arms, wrists), and the metal seemed to break up and dissolve. We gauged whether this was happening by whether their pain left and they regained mobility where the metal had previously prevented it. A few could no longer feel the screws, pins, plates, or the like under their skin.

A key learning point from all of this is that expectant faith seems to attract the presence of God, releasing even greater faith. It becomes like a "faith tornado" that increases in power as more and more happens. All in all, it was a good weekend in Adelaide. I am extremely encouraged by how the churches are coming together and by the level of excitement the Lord is stirring among His people. Let the kingdom come—even more powerfully and perceptibly.

June 17, 2014— Taipei, Taiwan

Taipei is a typical Asian city; the central business district is very well connected and modern, but outside, where the rest of humanity lives, is a warren of grimy multistory apartments (without elevators for the most part) sliced by fetid alleys and bordered by a thick tropical jungle that tumbles down to where the housing blocks begin. Temples and shrines abound, including on the sidewalks of what would be the equivalent of Park Avenue; you might see a place to kneel wedged next to the Benetton store, for instance, or in the underground parking lot.

They worship everything in Taiwan. Even though the country is nominally Buddhist, the people are also Taoist, Shinto, and several other religions I had not heard of before, including one called I-kuan-dao that seems to be a blend of five major religions, including Christianity. I have also seen shrines and statues erected "to an unknown God" (no kidding), just like what Paul found in Athens (Acts 17:23). Notwithstanding all of this, the people are friendly, and just as in other places, God is willing to back the proclamation of His kingdom.

We held meetings in Tainan on three successive days with progressively growing attendance. On day one, I preached on the kingdom of God out of Mark 1:14–15, and the Lord healed 100 percent of the people who came forward. I know that many, particularly in the West, doubt this can happen; it does, and it did in Tainan. Keep in mind this took place in a fairly Westernized Foursquare Church that had a theoretical belief in healing but hadn't seen very much of it. Many eyes widened as people were healed in plain view. The team that came with me from Los Angeles did an outstanding job of translating and being prayer partners.

During the second day, I preached on what happens when the Spirit comes, both theologically and phenomenologically. Every person who wanted prayer was touched. Not all were healed, but the few who weren't nonetheless improved significantly. On the third day, I presented an overview of the gifts of the Spirit at the pastor's request. More people attended than the previous two days, and again we had 100 percent healing. Some of these were people who had been partially healed on day two. This ably illustrates what Jerry has said about contending, pressing, and continuing to ask. God wants us to do this! He wants to do His work in us more than we want it. We just need to find and remove the obstacles here "on earth" that hinder healing from flowing "as in heaven."

We've seen considerable deliverance in Tainan, which should not be surprising in light of what I just described. One man had been inexplicably depressed for more than thirty years. His doctors had progressively increased his medication to no avail. However, he was becoming paralyzed from the medicine, or so he thought. One of my team is a licensed pharmacist in California, and she could not medically understand how a man on antidepressants could be paralyzed. She hypothesized that he was having undiagnosed strokes. (I can't confirm or deny this, but that was the considered opinion of someone we would normally view as a medical professional.) In any case, as we interviewed him through *two* interpreters since the language in Tainan isn't the normal Taiwanese my team speaks (in other words, English speaker → Mandarin speaker → Taiwanese speaker → Tainanese speaker → man), it became apparent that at age sixteen he had participated in an I-kuan-dao dedication ceremony. He'd had a "hole opened near the top of his forehead" (this was not literally true, but it was done in the spirit, not unlike what Hindus do with chakras). Shortly thereafter his depression began.

Through the interpreters we had him renounce the ceremony he had participated in all those years ago. Then we had him tell I-kuan-dao to leave, and we commanded it to leave. He manifested, heaved, slumped his shoulders, and looked up.

"It's gone!" he said.

"What's gone?"

"My depression. I feel light in my chest and my head."

"Anything else?"

"I don't know. I just feel different."

"Can you walk?"

He tried with some difficulty, so we rebuked the spirit of infirmity and commanded paralysis to leave. He began walking, at first with some awkwardness, but soon, with great ease and fluidity he was marching across the stage! The room erupted in applause. His wife broke down and fell to the floor, sobbing and laughing and saying something about Jesus in Tainanese. It was glorious! [Later, as we left to catch the train back to Taipei, we passed him on a scooter at one of the local street markets. He smiled, waved, and threw both hands in the air, making fists. I suppose this is a universal sign of victory.]

Meanwhile, a woman responded to a word of knowledge for problems with an eighteen-inch-long scar on her left shin. Her leg was healed, as was a back condition that had not been identified by word of knowledge. During this time of prayer, she was slain in the Spirit in front of the church. People stood up in amazement, chattering in Tainanese and pointing at her. Through a translator, she said she was experiencing numbness in her leg. A team member called me over to talk about this. Initially, it didn't concern me, as numbness can be a sign of healing, but something didn't feel right. So we told the numbness to go unless it was the Holy Spirit healing the leg. Then she began to cry and writhe, telling us it hurt badly. The team member looked at me, bewildered. I didn't know what it was either, so I waited and asked our Father what it was. I heard, "It is a Buddhist spirit."

I asked the translator to inquire if she was a first-generation Christian. She was, as was most of the congregation. So we had her renounce the spirit of Buddha, then she really began manifesting violently. Two team members took her into the next room for more prayer so I could continue the meeting. As they went, I asked them to break the power of the offerings she had made in Buddhist temples and to command the spirit to *come out!* Quite a commotion occurred in the next room for about thirty seconds, then they all came back into the sanctuary. The woman was beaming, and the team was smiling too! The pain was gone, the back was healed, the leg was healed, and a headache she had had her entire life had disappeared. Jesus had won again!

Here is a third story. A young woman received a considerable touch from the Lord on night one. She came wearing a yarmulke, and due to her style of dress (combat fatigues) and her US Marine Corps-style haircut, I mistook her for a young man. I even mistakenly addressed her in English as "him," but one of the team members corrected me, thankfully. She was seeking identity by following the Jewish law, which I found very odd here in Taiwan. (However, as noted, this is a very religiously diverse place.) She also received substantial inner healing that night, as she was alienated from her family, who she believed did not accept her. The pastor later told us she was one of his most troubled parishioners.

On day two, she came forward for more prayer. I had the interpreter ask her if she'd ever had any sexual contact with women and if she used porn. The interpreter looked horrified and didn't want to ask. I said if she was to get free, we needed answers to those questions. The girl nodded affirmatively and hung her head, adding, "It was just touch, nothing more." Her hands curled up as we have often seen in cases of sexual bondage—stiff fingers, almost clawlike, with the palms turned up and the arms rigid. [Sometimes the face contorts as well. The Bible tells us sin dwells in our members (Rom. 6:19). So when that sin, which often has a spirit attached to it, encounters the Holy Spirit, it rises to the surface and manifests in that kind of way before it breaks, and the person is freed. We see it over and over again. We also see it when people have anger issues.] We had her renounce the behavior and repent, then we pronounced forgiveness over her (John 20:21). We broke the bondage, then commanded the unclean spirits of pornography and lesbianism out. She coughed, retched, and shook. Then she looked up.

The change was astounding. When we left Tainan, she looked like a completely different person, except for the short haircut (hair does, after all, take time to grow). I left the pastor with instructions on care in the aftermath of deliverance, but it seemed clear that the kingdom of heaven had broken in over this young woman as well.

June 17, 2014—
Taipei

Today was busy. We had a leaders' meeting at a church, then headed to a meeting at the headquarters of a manufacturer of high-end computer devices, based in the "Silicon Valley" of Taipei. We had dinner with the CEO and his marketing director; it was one of the most phenomenal Chinese meals I have ever had. Forget everything you thought you knew about Chinese food; Taiwanese cuisine is the best. After fifteen courses, we walked over to the office for the meeting.

I won't soon forget that experience. The meeting was held in the boardroom, which could comfortably seat at least one hundred. Hanging on the wall of this gleaming white-and-gray space, all trimmed in steel and glass, was a *cross*! There were also characters painted on the wall dedicating the company to the glory of God. I'm pretty sure no one in the West has *ever* seen anything like that in the workplace; it tells you something about what is possible in Taipei versus the West. It also says something about the consecration of that CEO. The people in attendance ran the gamut from the CEO himself, to a woman who manages a top female athlete, to a man who had once been the leader of a large Chinese gang in California, to the general counsel of a large technology company.

There was also a man who is a top rap artist; he was dressed like Rick Nielsen, the lead guitarist from Cheap Trick. To say this was a mixed group would be a gross understatement, but the overall trend was "upmarket." After a short teaching, we prayed for this group of marketplace ministers, and the Lord touched them all.

One of the women had breast cancer and requested prayer. She fell over under the power of the Spirit, but what was more encouraging was the extreme heat and fire she felt on her chest. She said it was so hot she wanted to take off her blouse (she didn't)! Heat is usually a positive sign, but of course, there was no way to verify at that moment that she was healed. Nevertheless, everyone left with big smiles, chattering excitedly about how God had visited them that night.

June 18, 2014 (Morning)— Taipei

It is difficult to know where to begin. Today felt like we were living inside a Darren Wilson film (*Finger of God*, *Furious Love*, *Father of Lights*). Our morning meeting began with the converted gangster from yesterday and his twenty employees—all "working girls." He himself led them to the Lord following his own conversion, which had taken place two weeks earlier. They had traveled four hundred fifty kilometers to come to the meeting, and as soon as we walked in this morning, we knew it was a divine appointment.

I had prepared a message out of Luke 7:36–50 because I knew we would be pressed for time and I could teach this one in under five minutes. (Yes, it truly happened—and remember, I had to have it translated into Chinese, so I could only talk about two and a half minutes!) Here is a summary:

1. Jesus lets sinners come near to Him (7:38).

2. Jesus lets women come near to Him, which is a significant issue in male-dominated societies like ancient Israel or modern Taiwan (7:38).

3. Jesus sees our tears, and they don't offend Him (7:38, 44).

4. The love (devotion) forgiven people have for Jesus is a measure of how well they understand the forgiveness they have received (7:41–48).

5. Jesus has the power to forgive sin, and when He brings forgiveness, He also brings about healing in other areas of our lives (7:50).

Even before I finished speaking, the Holy Spirit was falling on the women and I was fighting back tears. The translator was also crying.

We had been asked to pray for all the women, and as I looked at my watch, I thought we had fourteen minutes before we had to be finished and out the door. Knowing that the women from Tainan had left before 6 a.m. to be here and that they needed to return, we prayed for them first. Six women lined up on one side of the room. We were about to pray when I felt a check in my spirit, so I asked if all of them were saved. Two were not. I asked if they would like to receive Christ. One wanted to, while the other was unsure.

So the translator prayed with the first woman, and as one friend of mine used to say, "She got saved *hard!*" She began sobbing deeply. The other women saw this, and before we could really say anything, the Holy Spirit descended on them all. They were shaking, crying, crashing to the floor, and falling on the couches in the room where we had gathered. Then He fell on the women from Taipei, and they were similarly swept up by the power of God. (He apparently didn't care from which city they had come, and He sovereignly broke the pastor's protocol. "As you wish, Lord!") Just then I asked which woman had the pain in the left side of her uterus and in her left ovary. One woman raised her hand in the midst of tears, and an amazing surge of power came over her body as she crashed to the floor. We learned later that she was healed in that moment.

As we prayed over the rest of the women, other words began to come forth from the team: fear, shame, uncleanness, perversion, rape, and more. Pandemonium broke out. Women were crying, falling, screaming, laughing, and shaking; and in the midst of it all, the love of the Father was enveloping them.

Then a word came forth about abortion. Nine hands went up sheepishly. We gathered these women in one group and prayed with them over the sin of ending their children's lives, and we spoke the Father's forgiveness over them. They were inwardly healed, delivered, and cleansed en masse in one of the most spectacular demonstrations of God's love anyone on the team had ever seen. I'm not sure how to describe what we saw, but God met these women!

While this was finishing, I looked over at the woman who had not wanted to receive Christ at first. I returned to her, laid my hands on her head, and asked the Father to open heaven over her as He had just done for those who'd had abortions. She crumpled and wept and wept and wept.

"You have a tightness in your chest that never goes away," I said. She nodded.

"And you are afraid of human touch, especially the touch of men." She went into overdrive, sobbing uncontrollably. I asked the translator to ask if she now wanted to receive Christ. Yes! Yes! Yes! So she too was born again this morning, and moments afterward, she was filled with the Spirit, speaking in tongues and being freed of that tightness and fear that had haunted her for years.

Around that time the gangster who had brought these girls repented for all he had done, both to and with them. Then he asked for prayer for the cancer that was eating his body, just as the spiritual cancer had eaten his soul. He had a large tumor in his nose and sinuses, with secondary tumors in his lungs, kidneys, and liver. He was knocked to the floor by the power of God and lay there moaning as power swept through him. He said he felt fire burning his face, throat, lungs, and abdomen. (Was he healed? There's no way to be sure, but he sure looked like he was getting healed.)

Then his younger lieutenant asked for prayer. He had wanted to die after a motorcycle accident damaged his spine three years ago; he had been in excruciating pain ever since. The team prayed for him once, and the pain level went down to a three or four. We then rebuked a Tao spirit and a Buddhist spirit, both of which came out with obvious manifestations, whereupon the power of God took the man to the floor. He was free!

While this was happening, several other words of knowledge came forth, and we had the women pray for their friends. I hate to tell the skeptics, but it was another 100 percent healing morning (with the possible exception of the gangster with cancer), and the last several healings were all conducted by the women. The team merely coached. Shoulders, hands, feet, and necks were all healed as newbies prayed.

At about this time, I looked at my watch; it was 10:30. We were thirty minutes over our time! Phones and cameras came out, and we quickly took photos, exchanged tearful hugs, and left. Moments later we were back on the streets of Taipei, wondering what had just happened. We feel privileged to have journeyed with Jesus this morning as He walked among these women who are (or more accurately, had been) outcasts. This was how He must have lived. It enraged the religious, but it brought the kingdom of God to Earth. My only regret is that we caught none of it on film as we had been asked not to film anything due to privacy concerns.

June 18, 2014 (Evening)— Taipei

Our next stop was a television studio with more than a thousand employees. We were to film and hold a meeting here. This is a Christian-owned station, but its programming is not purely Christian. The owner is currently in prison for past offenses, but his lieutenant had come to the Lord and then led her boss to faith. She is running the company while discipling her imprisoned boss! It is a complex story and unlike anything I have seen before.

We pulled up in front of a building that served as the headquarters of this television network. The woman who greeted us, Pastor Sue, runs the company's in-house chapel services and reports to the CEO. Yes you read that correctly. When the founder/owner came to the Lord, he hired Pastor Sue to serve as his personal chaplain and to oversee the spiritual life of the company. There is a chapel downstairs near the cafeteria that will comfortably seat a hundred and hold daily praise and prayer services. Large crosses prominently adorn the walls on each floor and the boardroom. One set of the key performance indicators that each manager must report on monthly deals with spiritual matters: Is gossip rising or falling? Have any come to the Lord in that work group? Have any been filled with the Holy Spirit? What healings or deliverances have occurred? What spiritual needs are people expressing? These are in addition to regular business metrics.

After lunch in the company cafeteria, we went into the chapel, where I spoke on miracles in the workplace from Acts 8:4–8. In response to a word of knowledge, a man came forward. We didn't know until later that he was an executive and dozens of people report to him. He had a sore right knee and upper leg that had given him periodic trouble for years. On camera (this was a TV studio after all), he received prayer twice for healing. He improved each time, but he wasn't fully healed.

After the meeting concluded, we talked with him further. He was a first-generation Christian. He had been involved in Buddhism and had been a temple guardian. He had also been involved in Taoism, I-kuan-dao, and ancestor worship. He had also been an assistant to a powerful medium. Though he was a Christian now, he had never had deliverance. We took him through prayers of renunciation of the sins of idolatry, ancestor worship, and necromancy. We had him renounce the spirits of each religion (including a guardian spirit from the Buddhist temple) as well as any power/benefit they brought, then we had him command them to leave. Next we commanded the demons to come out. His shoulders immediately hunched; he leaned forward, wheezed a couple of times, then coughed and fell forward under the power of God.

Can you imagine this happening in a company facility, let alone a chapel, while senior executives are looking on? When this man arose from the floor, he said he felt like he had been scrubbed on the inside: his vision was clearer and brighter, and his breathing was easier. Oh, and his leg was fully healed. I should have listened to my own sermon: Acts 8:5–7 states that Philip ministered deliverance *before* healing in the marketplace!

After a tour of the company facilities, the executives, including Pastor Sue, asked us for prophetic words about the individuals, their futures, and the company. We talked about the company's strategy, operations issues, and more. We shared not just prophetic words but also wisdom from experience and the Word of God. What really impressed me is how innovatively these Taiwanese Christians are seeking to bring the kingdom of God into the workplace and marketplace. They are genuinely seeking to reexamine church as it has been traditionally practiced and to begin embedding Christian meetings anywhere people gather and space can be located. The leaders of the move of God in Taipei are young and bold. They are well integrated into their society, yet they have not compromised their commitment to Christ, His church, or His cause. I have great confidence in what will happen here under their prayer-saturated, prophetically charged, Spirit-led leadership. From the low to the high, the kingdom of God really is advancing in Taipei—and if I sound a little excited, it's because I am.

June 21, 2014—
Taipei

We head home tomorrow evening. Two days ago we visited Fort Santo Domingo, which the Spanish established in 1628 to stop the advance of competing empires (principally Japan but also China and Korea) during colonial days. Not far from there, we visited Aletheia University, which is named for the Greek word for "truth." On its campus is a building called, improbably, "Oxford Hall." It is now a museum, but it was once the site of the first women's educational institution in northern Taiwan, founded by Rev. George Lesley Mackay.

Mackay was a Canadian Presbyterian of obviously Scottish descent. The Catholic Church established a few churches during the Spanish period, but Mackay is widely credited with bringing the gospel to Taiwan. He was born in 1844 and arrived in Taiwan in December 1871 at age twenty-seven. Within a year he had established both a church and a college. He was a dentist by training, and he ministered among the lowland Aborigines, later establishing a medical college as well. Still today Presbyterian churches in Taiwan, the largest Protestant church movement in the country, trace their descent from him. It is not an overstatement to say that if there had been no Rev. Mackay, Protestant Christianity might not exist in Taiwan. In fact, locally he is known as "the apostle of Taiwan."

One of the tribes Mackay evangelized was the Hakka, which at the time was at war with another tribe. As Mackay preached to them, the entire tribe came to Christ. This is strange to the Western ear because we are individualistic. However, Asian society in general is collective. If an influencer comes to faith, then his or her entire tribe will likely convert. This is what happened with the Hakka. Upon their conversion one of them put his life at risk by going to a hostile tribe, but he did so out of love for them and for Christ. He converted our host's grandfather, and with him, the tribe. The war ended, and our host's grandfather, father, and he himself became ministers of the gospel. Our host considers himself a spiritual grandchild of Mackay.

This story provides a very different view of apostleship than what is now widely touted in the West, but it sounds more biblical to me. Mackay ministered in signs and wonders, but these are not usually reported (particularly in Presbyterian history!); in fact, the stories are often suppressed. However, those who were part of that move of God know the truth. Now God is raising another move, and it is through men like our host, who is still the prince of his tribe (although he has not been back to them in many years and is, in fact, a very urbanized Taiwanese). Perhaps he and I will visit them together sometime in the future. He impresses me deeply, and in my short visit here, I have come to love him like a brother.

Last night I preached at his church. Hundreds, including many nonbelievers, came to receive prayer for healing. At the end of the evening, our host baptized four who came to Christ during the service, including a woman whose daughter had brought her for prayer. Some time ago this woman had a total knee replacement, and afterward, she became paralyzed from the neck down. This condition had gradually improved so that she had limited upper-body mobility, but she still suffered from total paralysis of the legs. Nobody could explain this condition, and doctors refused to see her. (Perhaps they feared being blamed for the paralysis or for not finding a cure.)

She came to the meeting in a wheelchair, but after hearing the message, she committed her life to Christ, was immediately healed, then *walked* up to the stage to be baptized! Initially, she needed support to walk, but by the time she came on stage, she was able to walk by herself, without assistance. I have photos of the woman before her healing, then as she was being healed and as she was baptized. Now *that* is what we are talking about! The kingdom of God is advancing in Taiwan!

June 22, 2014—
Taipei

Yesterday we held a training seminar for leaders. While this was underway, one of the team received a message from a pastor in Tainan stating that in the aftermath of our visit there, someone had come to his church seeking prayer. He excitedly reported that because of what he had learned during our visit, he prayed, and the person was healed! This was a major milestone for him.

Today was our last day here. We had a meeting this morning with a small group of people who are being discipled by our host. All of them are very influential in the business, entertainment, and legal communities. Because they attend other churches, none of them had been at the other meetings this week.

One man was a top snowboarder before he broke his leg several years ago, ending his career. He lost all sponsorships, fell into obscurity, and lingered in depression. To remedy his condition, doctors had surgically removed bone from his hip and transplanted it into his leg and ankle, but the procedure was only partially successful. Moreover, by now the bone transplant was breaking down, and he was losing the ability to walk. His wife asked us to pray for him. After evicting a Shinto, a Buddhist, and a "dog spirit" as well as driving off a familiar spirit from his deceased mother (as a Japanese practitioner of Shinto and Buddhism, the man had engaged in ancestor worship), he regained the use of his foot and leg, repeatedly testing it for flexibility, range of motion, and so on. All was normal, except for a mild, localized pain just below the ankle bone (level one out of ten). We couldn't seem to get that to leave, but whatever his bone condition had been, it was healed, and he could walk, jump, and run normally once again! It was a gratifying end to the trip.

July 7, 2014—
Los Angeles

We returned from Belize and southern Mexico last week. Belize is a former British colony in Central America that achieved independence in 1981. It bears the name of the former capital, Belize City, which remains a relic from when Belize was known as British Honduras. Belize has a Caribbean feel to it, and there is no question that you are in Central America when you are there; although English is widely spoken, most residents also speak Spanish. Like the region of southern Mexico we would travel to next, the population is heavily Mayan.

Our meetings were held in Belmopan, the national capital. To minimize cost, we all flew into Cancún, then caravanned south in a small bus and a passenger car. The border crossings were uneventful, but neither were they rapid. We drove all night (something we had not anticipated) and arrived at dawn. Consequently, the first day was spent sleeping or taking in a few sights before the meetings began that evening.

While we were there, we met with the head of the nation's largest independent television network (the rest being controlled by the government for propaganda) as well as with the representative of the Roman Catholic Primate—the lead bishop of the country.

We learned that the Obama administration has been applying great pressure to the government to comply with its plans for "fundamental change" in Belizean society. Specifically, this means trying to mainstream gay rights of all kinds, with many things promised for compliance and many things threatened to be withdrawn or withheld for noncompliance. The administration views

Belize as the salient point in the region, where change can happen most rapidly. From there, it is believed that the rest of Central America will fall into line with the administration's objectives. Why the US government has made such social change and meddling in the internal affairs of a sovereign nation the centerpiece of its foreign policy is anyone's guess, but it just isn't happening in Belize. Incidentally, this is a global effort the administration is putting forth, and it explains in part why such initiatives seem to be gaining rapid acceptance.

Other nations, including those in Oceania, have come under similar pressure. Recently, however, the governments of Kenya and Uganda politely but firmly told the Obama administration to cease and desist with such efforts. As far as Central America goes, apparently Yankee "gunboat" diplomacy isn't really a thing of the past. I was embarrassed that my government would be making this the focus of its foreign policy in this land.

The meetings in Belize were well attended, albeit somewhat smaller and with a different mix than we had been led to expect. During our extended driving times from and back to Mexico, the Holy Spirit fell in the small bus and nearly all the team members found themselves activated in things they had not previously experienced; this included seeing angels, one person seeing Jesus, several experiencing open visions and trances, and many experiencing inner healing and deliverance. Consequently, when the team rolled into ministry time, things were happening quite powerfully and rapidly.

I lost track of the number of demons we drove out that were tied to the worship of ancient Mayan deities, but it was a considerable number. Syncretism (participation in two or more religions, in this case Christianity and Mayan rituals) is alive and well in many parts of the world. Almost everywhere we go, we need to lead people through deliverance for their participation in what cannot be called anything other than idol worship along with

Christianity. People were also set free from the kinds of spirits you might find anywhere (rejection, anxiety, gluttony, drunkenness, and so on), and we ministered to quite a few who had been prostitutes (or still were) as well as to homosexuals. All of these people found great freedom.

I was surprised to find that our old nemesis Freemasonry was widespread in Belize, derived from the country's British roots. Although I had not anticipated this, once I knew it was common, we started dealing with it. The takeaway for me was, "Never take anything for granted." One woman had a *very* demonstrable and loud deliverance from Freemasonry, and she was thereby healed of a female disorder as well as knee and back problems when the spirits were driven out. We also led a few people to Christ. The leaders in Belize have invited us to return, and I look forward to seeing what else may transpire on our second trip.

We left Belize and headed back into Mexico, to a town called José María Morelos (JMM). This is a district capital (not a provincial capital) in the heart of La Zona Maya (the Mayan Zone). The people there all look very Mayan, and traces of that civilization are everywhere. It is also clear that many of the old practices persist. At one point we visited a sinkhole (called a *cenote* in Spanish) to swim, and the locals told us that formerly, virgins were thrown into it to appease the water gods there. We saw the faint tracings of child-sized bodies on the flat tablelike rocks where etchings had been made over and over through the centuries, like a chalk outline at a crime scene, until the etchings became permanent. The children would have been bound and placed on the rock ledge about two hundred feet above the water before they were thrown in.

While we were at the *cenote*, one of our local team members who had been converted on our last trip requested baptism. It seemed a suitable offset to the evil that had taken place there in centuries past.

The next day we returned to Cancún and quickly organized a meeting there. The Lord moved, with one man healed of a neck condition he'd had since a television set fell on his head ten years previously. He'd had prayer before, but when we commanded the trauma to leave, the pain left his body and he wept openly as he regained mobility in his neck, shoulders, and arms. This happened in front of the entire room, so there were many witnesses.

July 7, 2014—
Los Angeles

Tonight I was on a Skype call with a friend in Asia. He just returned from a ministry trip in Krabi and Phuket, Thailand. While he was there, he did not go into any temples or eat any food sacrificed to idols. He was working at a retreat and generally kept a low profile. Nevertheless, he was having difficulty breathing, and his energy level was very low. He said the doctors suspected chronic fatigue, but he could point to no particular causes. I said, "Then it must be a spirit."

I googled "Phuket Thailand local gods" and looked at the images. Try it. You will be shocked at the many pictures of people in full demonic manifestation, including with their eyes rolled back, walking on fire, piercing and cutting themselves with swords, lances, and axes. Those pictures explain better than I ever could why I teach as I do about tattooing, piercing, and cutting. It doesn't matter whether you have a big tattoo or a small one, something from the Bible or something demonic; tattoos by their nature violate the sanctity of the body and draw blood, as forbidden in Leviticus 19:28.

[Many will say this is "Old Testament" and doesn't matter, but a close reading of the Mosaic Code shows it dealt with the civic administration of ancient Israel, the Temple ritual, and morals. The civic code of Old Israel no longer applies as that nation no longer exists, but modern Israel has imported what it can from the ancient code into its modern apparatus. The Temple ritual likewise no longer applies because the Temple no longer exists, and Jesus' sacrifice takes the place that all sacrifices were intended to provide. But Paul fully restates the moral code in his writings in the context of how Christians should live. The language about tattoos falls under the moral code of the Mosaic Law and could be broadly subsumed under the prohibition of shedding and eating blood found in Acts 15:20 and 29 as well as Acts 21:25.]

Still on the phone with my friend, I asked if he had been feeling or seeing anything, and he said, "I see something that looks like a Hindu god, but Thailand is a Buddhist country." I soon found an image of Wat Chalong. A wat is a temple, so I surmised that the god's name must be Chalong. At that point I said, "Chalong, come out!" My friend immediately went into a full-scale demonic manifestation, coughing, retching, and hacking. Presently it cleared, and he felt somewhat better. He also said he felt something detach from the back of his head.

As I scanned more images, I saw several people who had pierced their cheeks with swords, needles, even gun barrels! So I asked my friend if he had any unusual feelings in his cheeks. He said, "Yes, I had some tingling on one side, but as you asked about it, it moved to the other cheek." He asked if there was anything on the internet dealing with monkeys, and I found a couple of images of monkeys from the area. One source said monkeys were sacred, and one was called "Ibonito." So on a hunch, I said, "Spirit of Ibonito, come out!" My friend began vomiting, coughing, and expelling a great quantity of ejecta. He also saw an image of a monkey as the spirit was leaving. The sensation in his cheeks left as well.

Another image caught my attention, this one of a dark god with red eyes. It is the spirit of darkness over the whole of Thailand, and its name is Phra Rahu. I said, "Let's just check something.

Phra Rahu, if you are there, make your presence known and come out!" At this my friend said he could feel something both inside and attached to the exterior of his back and chest. I told it to leave immediately. Again my friend began manifesting heavily, coughing, retching, and falling to the ground. He said he felt like an octopus was releasing its tentacles from him, like suction cups detaching. He had a sense of the room spinning around him, and he almost lost consciousness.

When he regained his senses, I commanded the spirit of chronic fatigue to come out, and again there was a heavy manifestation. When it subsided, I said, "If there are any other Thai spirits here, I command you in Jesus' name to leave my friend and never return!" He began coughing and vomiting again; after a couple of minutes, this subsided. He said he felt several weaker spirits leave in response to that last command. I checked for a couple of other spirits that I had seen come up in my Google search, but nothing happened, so we concluded that he was probably not afflicted by these (thankfully). My friend said he felt like his strength had returned to normal. He tested it several times, and all seemed well.

I know this will stretch some of you; it did me. However, this is the nature of pagan idolatry and the power of demons. Rituals of the type I've just described occur in nearly every nation of the world—Indonesia, Taiwan, Mexico, and others. The names change, and the functions may change slightly, but the overall effect is the same.

Because of our secularized Western worldview, we struggle to acknowledge what is clearly described and condemned in Scripture. As I said, if you have questions, search the exact phrases I have just posted. Many people suffer from incurable and unexplainable diseases and afflictions rooted in demonic oppression. That is not to say we should simply go about rebuking into the air or labeling everything we don't understand as a demon. A little knowledge can be a dangerous thing. Deliverance is a targeted activity by which we engage the enemy as he holds and torments a human host. My friend was healed from more than ten thousand miles away because it *was* demonic, and we called the demons out by name. Let's not deny what Scripture affirms. When deliverance is needed, nothing else will do: not intercession, not inner healing, not good intent, not kindness, not compassion.

"The reason the Son of God appeared was to destroy the works of the devil" (1 John 3:8).

July 23, 2014—
Launceston, Tasmania

While I was praying yesterday morning, I was thinking about Hebrews 13:3: "Remember those who are in prison, as though in prison with them, and those who are mistreated, since you also are in the body." I have also been thinking about this passage from Hebrews:

> Some were tortured, refusing to accept release, so that they might rise again to a better life. Others suffered mocking and flogging, and even chains and imprisonment. They were stoned, they were sawn in two, they were killed with the sword. They went about in skins of sheep and goats, destitute, afflicted, mistreated—of whom the world was not worthy—wandering about in deserts and mountains, and in dens and caves of the earth.
>
> —HEBREWS 11:35–38

The last week has brought a shocking, horrifying, saddening flood of news about atrocities committed by a group called ISIS against our brothers and sisters in Iraq and (this morning) in Syria, where nine people were crucified and babies were shot and their bodies thrown into a pit. Homes and businesses of Christians are having an Arabic "N" spray-painted on them (for Nazarene), then the ISIS fighters take the property for the funding of the new Islamic caliphate. They kill the owners if they won't convert, or they place them under a condition called *dhimmi* (second-class citizenship) and subject them to a high punitive tax, called *jizyah*, which encumbers them economically forever. The plight of Iraqi and Palestinian Christians has similarly been ongoing for years but seldom publicized. However, the cumulative effect has been the almost complete depopulation of areas (provinces and countries, not mere neighborhoods) that have long been inhabited by Christians. This is far more than merely picking up and moving to a new city, as we in the West do so easily. It involves the loss of homes, lands, and businesses that have in many cases been in the family for centuries. It may involve emigration, if they can find a country to accept them. Furthermore, it involves the loss of a culture, including the holy sites and shrines these Christians tend out of devotion to the acts of God in history.

This is difficult for Westerners to grasp because much of our faith experience comes through biblical exposition and perhaps encounters with the Holy Spirit. Our faith has a noetic, cognitive bent to it. In many of these lands, however, their history and faith are inextricably linked. To destroy their history is to seek the obliteration of the faith they have carried for centuries. The tombs of the prophets Jonah, Nahum, and Ezekiel have all been desecrated in the last week. Many wives and daughters have been taken as "wives" for *mujahideen*. This is persecution on a systemic scale. It is planned, intentional evil.

As if all of this weren't enough, yesterday brought news of a new wave of arrests, church desecration, and property confiscation in China. Of course, the popular image of modern China would suggest that persecution is over and that China has become another free-market country. Hence, all should be forgiven and forgotten. Yet under Mao Zedong, well over fifty million (and that is a *very* conservative number) believers and other undesirables were tortured and killed. That is more than twice the entire population of Australia and more than the combined populations of California, Arizona, and Nevada. The level and intensity of persecution in modern China may be reduced, perhaps, but it does not negate the fact that people are being jailed for their beliefs. Their churches are being bulldozed. Their bodies are being bruised and broken. Their families are subjected to intense economic and physical suffering and deprivation. Children are being orphaned and left to fend for themselves. I might add that anyone who has even a rudimentary understanding of inner healing will immediately see that the destruction isn't just being wrought on this generation; the trauma will be passed down to the children and grandchildren of those so treated.

These latest incidents have been highly publicized, most likely due to their shock appeal, but believers in other countries have been suffering on an ongoing basis without the benefit of any similar media frenzy. Think of the persecuted Christians of Somalia, Ethiopia, and Nigeria, for example, who have been bombed by their own government, shot, starved, raped, and more.

Why am I talking about all of this? Because the Bible commands us to "remember those who are in prison, as though in prison with them, and those who are mistreated, since you also are in the body." We are called to sympathize, to empathize. We may be called upon by the Lord to support or to act on behalf of the persecuted.

And the same could happen here.

[There is something about empathizing with other believers that releases to us a great grace for this kind of miraculous life. We are called to love and appreciate the whole body of Christ, even though we may profoundly disagree with parts of it. That's very difficult because we believe firmly what we believe, and others are going diametrically opposite to it—but again we have to love them. When we let love for our brothers shrivel up in our hearts, how can we love God, whom we have not seen?]

The pressure being brought to bear on the churches of the West is not yet to the level I have just described, so to suggest an equivalence between the Middle East or China and the West would be absurd. Nevertheless, the power of secularism, often with government and other institutions behind it, is being brought to bear against people of faith in every Western nation. If their faith contradicts the dictates of these powers, they may be denied contracts. They may be denied employment or discharged from their jobs. They may be harassed through random searches and audits for no good reason. They may be sent for re-education (don't laugh; this recently happened in New Mexico). They may be denied promotions or kept from attaining academic positions (all of this is currently happening on a widespread scale in the West, particularly in the military). If you do the research, you will see I'm not exaggerating.

All of this leads me to ask: Could it be that a great persecution of the church is currently underway? (See Acts 8:1.) Please do not mistake me; I do *not* mean *the* Great Persecution or *the* Great Tribulation. Throughout history, there have been periods of persecution against the church. Some believers have been imprisoned unjustly, some have lost property, some have lost their purity, some have lost their lives. It seems to me, looking across the earth, that this is just such a time, albeit (said again for emphasis) *not the Great Tribulation*. Many have been crying out for the church to advance, but history shows us that most of the great advances of the church have come during times of distress and hardship. I am thrilled by all that the Lord is doing as I travel and hear reports from others. However, I think we all would do well to take sober stock and understand that we must be steadfast in the faith, despite difficulty, for it is "through many tribulations we must enter the kingdom of God" (Acts 14:22). John Wimber used to say, "We didn't get in cheaply; they won't either."

Here are a few other things to keep in mind:

1. We are not to return violence for violence. In the past, Christians have made this mistake, and the legacy haunts us to this day. (See Matthew 5:38–41.)

2. The peace we have known in the West is *not* the normal state of affairs for Christians. We should be thankful for it and seek to preserve it, but we must recognize that it only takes one evil ruler to change what we so easily take for granted. (See Romans 13:1 and 1 Peter 2:21–23.)

3. We are to pray for kings and all those in authority (presidents, prime ministers, cabinets, senators, representatives, judges) so that we may live peaceful and quiet lives, godly and dignified in every way. (See 1 Timothy 2:2.)

4. We must remember that s/he who endures to the end will be saved. Christianity is not a self-improvement program; it is a life of sacrifice. It is not a sprint; it is a marathon, so plan and prepare for the long haul. (See Matthew 24:13.)

5. Therefore "this means that God's holy people must endure persecution patiently, obeying his commands and maintaining their faith in Jesus." (See Revelation 14:12, NLT.)

Rise up, O [saints] of God!
Have done with lesser things;
Give heart and soul and mind and strength
To serve the King of kings.[2]

—William P. Merrill

August 18, 2014—
Perth, Western Australia

I arrived last night after spending most of the last four days in Esperance, a small Western Australian town of about fourteen thousand on the coast of the Southern Ocean. Esperance may well be the most beautiful place I have visited in Australia.

On Friday night, something pretty close to "the Toronto Blessing" fell in the room, and there was not only "holy laughter" but one woman was making laps around the church looking for all the world as though she were cantering on a horse! To be clear, I neither encourage nor incite this kind of behavior, and this particular woman is known for her sober and proper demeanor. However, this *was*, in fact, a work of the Holy Spirit in her. It was a blessing to watch, even if I did chuckle a bit. During the ministry time Saturday night, a holy hush fell on the room and people began interceding aloud for Esperance, the region, and the state of Western Australia. Many tears flowed, and some began publicly confessing their sins, including arrogance, pride, trying to control God, religious traditionalism, and anger. Near the end, a wave of the Holy Spirit crashed in on the room, releasing impartation over the group.

Three healings stand out in my mind. The first took place on Saturday night, when a teenage girl asked for prayer for her arm, which was paralyzed and causing her great pain. This pain had come about inexplicably just before the conference began. We had prayed unsuccessfully for her on Friday; on Saturday she returned for additional ministry. I asked her mother about Freemasons in the family. You guessed it: the girl's great-grandfather had been one. When we dealt with the Freemasonry, the paralyzing pain left for good. She was still fine on Sunday.

The next healing was for a woman who had tick fever some years ago. She had been bitten while in Bali and had suffered with neuralgia for many years as a result. In fact, it was more than neuralgia; it was a whole-body ache that had her on the verge (or over the edge) of tears most of the time. The Scriptures say that when Jesus healed Peter's mother-in-law of a fever, He "rebuked" it (Luke 4:39), which is language that elsewhere in Scripture describes how He handled evil spirits. So I took the woman's hands, invoked the kingdom of God over her, and rebuked both her pains and the tick fever, commanding them to leave. The ensuing manifestation was pronounced: she buckled and fell to the floor. When she arose, she was weeping uncontrollably, laughing and praising God. She threw her arms around my neck, thanking me profusely and declaring publicly that for the first time in over a decade she was pain free! She followed me around Sunday as I prayed for other people, offering to bring me coffee or tea and generally enjoying her new lease on life.

It is common in my travels to be challenged by people who believe we glorify God in our suffering. It is undoubtedly true that we can glorify God by suffering with patience and dignity rather than blaspheming and throwing a bedpan across the room. However, the greater glory comes when people are healed, as they never hesitate to credit God for His goodness. Moreover, when it happens in the midst of a community where the person's condition is well known, it causes the onlookers to glorify God as well—explicitly, aloud, and publicly. Several Scriptures demonstrate this, and I would encourage everyone to familiarize themselves with these verses so they can answer those who believe God wants His people to suffer. Healing is inextricably tied to the proclamation of the kingdom, as it demonstrates that God truly has come to the aid of His people. (See Matthew 9:35.) For

Scriptures on healing bringing glory to God, see Matthew 9:8; 15:31; Mark 2:12; Luke 5:26; 7:16; 13:13; 17:15; and John 11:4; 11:40.

The last healing was of a woman with arthritis. Several years ago, she and her husband had been missionaries with a mainline denomination. Somewhere along the line, they had become interested in the things of the Spirit, then found themselves in the awkward place of being told either to resign or be forced out after more than twenty years of service. It was an incredibly difficult time for them as they had to separate from longtime friends. Some former friends even went so far as to cross the street to avoid them.

In the intervening years, many of the broken relationships had somehow been restored, and this woman had also received a great deal of ministry over this series of interrelated experiences, but her arthritis only worsened. Among other things, she'd had her knees replaced with a caution never to kneel again. Also her hands and spine were severely afflicted, resulting in deformity and constant pain. I talked with her for several minutes about those who had mistreated her and her husband, primarily to satisfy myself that there was nothing more to be done in the area of forgiveness.

Forgiveness is a necessary first step for healing in cases like this, but many people stop there, believing it is the "one size fits all answer" to the affliction. The inevitable result is that people who have legitimately forgiven their offenders are sometimes bludgeoned by well-meaning Christians who urge them repeatedly to forgive them again. Convinced that there wasn't really anything further to be done in this area, when we began praying, I focused on the experience of having been shunned, and I broke the power of the "shunning spirit" over her. I also broke the power of the words spoken against her and her husband because, contrary to popular opinion, words do, in fact, have power. (See Proverbs 12:18, "There is one whose rash words are like sword thrusts, but the tongue of the wise brings healing.") She fell *to her knees*, weeping, laughing, crying, shaking, and moaning, and lay on the floor for several minutes. When she arose, all the pain in her body had left. She was free.

Esperance is a town whose name means "hope." The Lord brought hope to Esperance this weekend.

September 21, 2014— Bohemia, New York

I am writing from the Eastern United States, where I am on the front end of a trip that will take me south to Washington, DC, by way of Pennsylvania. I spent six of eight weeks in Australia in July, August, and early September. I love the people and the nation of Australia, but I must admit I returned home exhausted from this extended time away. I am now starting to feel revived, but it has taken some time to get there. The last trip to Australia was focused on the state of Western Australia, where I visited, among other places, Esperance, Wagin, Busselton, Bunbury, Mandurah, and Geraldton.

I often give testimonies of my journeys, and I have several I could share. However, the testimony I most want to share now is my own.

When I arrived in Australia, I had a small, hard lump in the palm of my left hand. Over several days it became larger and more painful, until it was highly inflamed and had swollen to the size of a large lima bean. I emailed my doctor, asking him to schedule an appointment for the day I got home so I could have it examined and possibly excised. I couldn't even pick up my baggage due to the sensitivity.

One night about halfway through the trip, I was teaching in Busselton/Yallingup, and the Lord was moving on the group. People were shaking, falling, crying…you know, generally getting blasted in the Spirit. In the midst of this, someone suggested they pray for my hand. Several people prayed earnestly. Seemingly nothing happened, but at least we tried. Yet progressively, over the next two weeks, the lump shrank, and by the time I got home it was nearly gone. I have continued checking, and a few days ago I could say it was in fact fully *gone*! I don't know where it went, but it isn't in my hand any longer! So I am here to give thanks to the Lord and to the group that prayed and testify that this obvious growth/tumor has literally dematerialized/vanished! Thank You, Jesus!

Some healings are instantaneous, and some are progressive. This is why the New Testament uses three words for healing: *therapeuo*, *iaomai*, and *sozo*. Each has its own meaning, roughly: healed (of a sickness), cured (of a disease, and often with an underlying complication that is more than physical), and comprehensively healed in multiple dimensions (soul, spirit, body). Biblical healing need not always be instantaneous, even though I'd prefer it. However, I'll take progressive healing if instantaneous healing isn't on offer. In this case, I didn't need to wait long for the healing to be completed, and I'm delighted to be able to give this public testimony.

October 18, 2014— Colombo, Sri Lanka

Things started well last night here in the capital city. Despite driving rain and traffic jams of biblical proportions, we had an overflowing, standing-room-only crowd. In fact, the traffic was so bad that I was picked up nearly forty-five minutes after the meeting had started, despite the agreed-upon plan to leave for the meeting an hour in advance. We finally made it to the church, where the crowd was in the midst of rich worship. When I walked in, it felt as though I had walked into a wall of God's presence. It seemed clear that we were in for a good night, despite the challenges getting there.

I spoke on "What Is the Gospel?" and then ministry began with seven people coming forward in response to a word of knowledge about shoulders. A couple of these people were called out of the crowd, while the others simply came forward in response to the

Word. In front of the room, all seven were healed, starting the night off with 100 percent healing. To be clear, six were healed all the way, while the seventh was about 75 percent healed. The first six demonstrated their healings and gave public testimony to them. The seventh, though, was an unusual case.

The man had been brutally beaten by four men thirteen years ago. In the aftermath of the attack, doctors had surgically removed tendons and ligaments from the man's shoulder, making it impossible for him to move his arm. In fact, as we began to pray, he said he was afraid to try anything because it would result in his arm popping out of the socket and a trip to the hospital. After receiving two rounds of prayer, he moved his arm three hundred sixty degrees as well as up and down. The only limitation: he could not reach directly up. The longer we prayed, though, the more his mobility increased, and it was still increasing as he left last night. I wouldn't be surprised if his arm is functioning at 100 percent this morning. This man is well known to the church, so his healing had a particular impact on the crowd—including on his wife, who looked on, sobbing, as God touched her husband.

This man had received prayer in the past but to no avail. In this instance, his healing came when I asked whether he had forgiven his attackers. When he did, the Spirit touched him powerfully; he fell backward dramatically and rested on the floor for about twenty minutes before rising, healed.

Another of the seven had similarly sought healing for her arm in the past but without success. When I asked whether she was a first-generation Christian, she stated that she was. I then asked about her family's religious background, and she said they had been Hindu. When I asked who was the god to whom she had been dedicated (not unlike the phenomenon of patron saints in Catholicism), she said, "Saraswati." So I had her renounce her dedication to this deity and tell it to leave her. When I subsequently commanded this spirit to release her and depart, she was instantly healed!

Later we had a general call for prayer, and with the exception of two who will return for more prayer today (rather than having to pray late into the night), 100 percent of the people who came forward also received full healings.

One situation was particularly noteworthy: a young woman was powerfully delivered from demons that shrieked, howled, and thrashed about on the floor. It was a short contest, though, as the Lord dispatched these invaders and vanquished several physical ailments in the process. Her breathing allergies all cleared completely in the wake of her deliverance. I expect that when she returns today, she will testify to having been healed of allergies to cheese and chocolate as well—and since we will live on cheese, chocolate, and french fries in heaven, she will now be ready to depart whenever the Lord sees fit to call her. (Yes, that is a joke!)

Finally, the pastor's two daughters were among those who came forward for prayer. Both are exceptionally consecrated young ladies, with great hunger for the Lord. They came asking that He use them in this city and in their generation. The Spirit of God fell on them powerfully.

October 19, 2014— Colombo

It is Sunday morning here as I write this. We had two sessions scheduled yesterday; the meeting ran from 9 a.m. to 9 p.m., and some people were still awaiting prayer when we left.

One of the highlights was talking with the woman who had been delivered the previous day. At lunchtime, she told me she had eaten some chocolate early in the morning. I asked how her body was reacting, and she said, "No reactions." As we were driving home last night, the pastor told me the woman had continued eating chocolate with no side effects. She brought her fiancé for prayer yesterday evening, and he was healed of a longstanding injury to his back and right leg. This morning's session saw 100 percent healing, and the afternoon session was the same, minus the one.

Additionally, the wife of the man whose tendons and ligaments had been surgically removed from his arm came for prayer. She told me he was now 100 percent healed, so what had begun the night before, Jesus completed overnight. This woman requested prayer for a series of health conditions, including a recurring headache that almost completely debilitated her at times. She also suffered from body pains that would assail her regularly, and reactions to various kinds of food and fragrances.

Shortly after I arrived on Thursday night, our hosts had asked if we could make time to pray for this woman. At some point in that discussion, they mentioned her name. It was very similar (but not identical) to the name of a specific Hindu god I have run into previously.

When the woman came for prayer, I recognized her name. Once she was delivered of that Hindu spirit, she was knocked to the floor and lay there weeping for several minutes. When she rose, she was completely healed of all of her symptoms, although she was still woozy from the power of the Holy Spirit on her. I laid hands on her a second time, praying for healing in her body and restoration for the lost years, and she fell to the ground again, this time for a considerably longer period. When she left the meeting last night, her face was radiant with the transformation the Lord had wrought within her. Between the healings of her husband's arm and her own conditions, salvation truly came to that household this weekend.

I love telling the stories of what Jesus does in these meetings, and it is tremendous when everyone gets healed. However, there is that minority of people who sometimes aren't immediately healed. This bothers me considerably, both because of the disappointment those people feel and because of the hardship they must continue to endure. All I can do in those instances is continue pressing the

Lord for answers to their healings. This morning, before I wrote this post or ate breakfast, I was asking the Lord for the key to that one healing the woman did not receive yesterday. I believe it is God's will to heal her, and I believe He will receive far more glory when she is healed than if she remains as she is.

October 22, 2014— Colombo

I finished up in Colombo tonight, and early tomorrow I head to Kegalle (pronounced "kay-gall"). Sunday night there was a meeting in the suburb of Ratmalana. Several hundred people attended, *all* of whom seemed to want prayer. A high percentage were healed in that meeting through words of knowledge and standing for prayer. Then the rest rushed the stage!

Both last night's and tonight's meetings were also well attended. Last night we met at the Tourist Board Hall in the central business district, and the audience included many business leaders. Among others, I prayed for four CEOs. During tonight's ministry time, a large number of people came forward for prayer. One of them was seventy-year-old PB, who fell three weeks ago in his bathroom, breaking his back (hairline fracture observable by X-ray). He lay on the floor for more than eighteen hours before someone came home and found him. He had been unable to pull himself up or crawl out of the bathroom due to the injury, which had, among other things, resulted in lost sensation and paralysis in both legs and feet. As of last night, he was still unable to walk.

I prayed for him for less than five minutes before asking him how his legs and feet felt. He said they felt "normal" with none of the symptoms he'd had before. When I asked if he wanted to try walking again, he said yes. This was one happy man, and he left pushing his own wheelchair out the door!

One of the things that has become very clear here in Sri Lanka is the need for deliverance ahead of many of the healings that are occurring. Sri Lanka is Buddhist country, so Buddhist spirits are the most common. However, there are also Hindu spirits due to India's proximity and the consequent minority Hindu population. Additionally, there is a large shrine in this city to Saint Anthony of Padua. Many of the believers here have Catholic backgrounds, and a significant percentage of them have been devoted to Saint Anthony and to what many scholars call "the cult of the saints." Moreover, many claim Saint Anthony as their patron saint.

Once these spirits—whether Buddhist, Hindu, or Catholic—are dealt with, well over 75 percent of the people are healed immediately. In a smaller percentage of cases, additional prayer (often simple healing prayer) is necessary before the healing happens. In PB's case, there was no need for deliverance because his was a purely physical healing of damage caused by the fall.

Something I've known for some time, but which has become especially clear after visiting eight countries in relatively rapid succession this year, is the commonality of the human condition. It is true that Sri Lanka isn't Taiwan isn't Indonesia isn't Australia isn't Mexico, but the problems people face (e.g., unstable employment, workplace harassment, domestic violence, sexual immorality, rejection, fear, unbelief, witchcraft, and death) are similar across societies. Moreover, the problems with demonic roots often reveal themselves through suspiciously similar characteristics, even across different languages, countries, and cultures. This is because archetypes, or ruling spirits, operate in essentially the same way; the names may change from culture to culture, but the functions are surprisingly similar. Thus, being effective when entering a new culture requires knowing the common areas of struggle along with the spirits that tend to be active in those struggles. Once this is understood, it leads to a much clearer "blueprint" (or mental map) of the enemy's strategies and consequently a more rapid ability to minister effectively in that new context.

Though a culture may be unfamiliar, it is often possible to discern which spirits may be operating by identifying other spirits they resemble based on previous experiences in other cultures. I do, of course, recognize that effective cross-cultural ministry involves much more than simply understanding this one spiritual dynamic. However, I'm highlighting this point because it is one of the keys that is so often overlooked. Without this understanding, it is possible to grasp all other cultural nuances and still not release the power of God into a region.

On a separate note, tonight, several Buddhists came forward for prayer. They didn't really know much about Christianity other than what I had shared. However, they needed something from God, and they were captivated by the healings they observed. I prayed with three to receive the Lord before we finally left after three hours of ministry time for a late dinner.

October 26, 2014—
Kandy, Sri Lanka

After Colombo, I went on to Kegalle, where we held a basic healing conference over two days. These meetings were held in a large public auditorium located above the post office, and several hundred people attended. We had some impressive healings, including people with frozen shoulders, paralyzed backs, lower-body paralysis, and skin conditions.

Kegalle is home to a sanctuary for orphaned elephants, and in one case, I had to drive out an "elephant spirit" before a person could receive her healing. Because the elephants bring tourist money to the town, some locals also worship them—hence the "elephant spirit" bondage. Worship of anything other than God Himself opens one up to spirits, as anyone who has ministered or traveled in this land will readily tell you. In the West, ministries often fail to take this into account because for several centuries Christian worship has been overwhelmingly dominant. That is now changing, so my experience here is a useful lesson to apply back home as well.

October 28, 2014—
Colombo

I will be leaving Sri Lanka tonight after two very full and tiring weeks in this beautiful country. I learned many, many lessons, and I am very thankful to the Lord for all that has transpired. I will briefly describe some of the significant healings that occurred in just the past week:

1. A woman who was partially blind with some kind of weblike obstruction over her eyes was healed nearly instantaneously. She is still healed as I type this. Hers is one of the healings I have on video.

2. A man with Parkinson's disease was healed in Kandy on Sunday. This is the first case of Parkinson's I have seen healed, but if it follows past patterns, more are to come. I have come to expect that once the first case of [insert malady here] is healed, subsequent healings come rather quickly and easily. I have a video testimony from this man.

3. A man in his late twenties with renal failure appears to have been healed Sunday in Kandy. He goes on dialysis every five days, so I will have a medical report shortly. His was a complex history, but having a baseline understanding of the kidneys often being a repository for anger (whether the person's own or anger directed at them) was the key to his healing. His mother *also* received a significant inner healing, as mother and son stepped

into some kind of "whirlwind of the Holy Spirit" that consumed them both.

4. A doctor educated in Britain was healed of an auto-immune disorder that was making her organs hard as a rock and causing fibers to form within her body. She was treating herself because no one in the country had the knowledge to help her. As a result, not only were her organs shutting down, but she could neither breathe properly nor swallow. She feared imminent death. When we prayed for her, her organs instantly became soft again, which was easily measured when she pressed on her abdomen. She returned two days later saying she had run tests on her own blood afterward and declaring that she was healed, able both to breathe and swallow.

5. A woman with severe, debilitating asthma was healed. She testified that she can now walk, cook, take care of the house, and function normally. Nobody had been able to help her before Jesus did. This woman is an elder in the church.

These are just a few samples of the healings that occurred. The Lord is good, and His love endures forever!

November 26, 2014—Los Angeles

I arrived home yesterday from my fifth trip to Australia this year—the sixty-eighth since I first went in the early 1990s. That is a lot of trips to Australia!

Last weekend was spent south of Melbourne, at a Baptist church in Victoria currently pastored by a former Anglican priest. I taught on prophecy—and based on the surveys people completed, my material was well received and they would welcome another such event in 2015. Prophecy seminars usually don't have as many healing stories as healing conferences (Ya think?!), but this was certainly an unusual and enjoyable conference. *Three* times during my teaching, the scent (a distinct smell) of the Lord came into the room. The first time, I paused the teaching to ask how many people could smell it. It was vaguely like frangipane or possibly jasmine. A few could detect it, so I invited all present who had never smelled the scent of the Lord to come forward. Virtually everyone who did so could smell it! (To be clear, before I did that, I surreptitiously sniffed a number of people to make certain that I wasn't simply smelling someone's cologne. I wasn't.)

The fragrance's impact on the crowd was electric, especially since so many had never experienced a "real," objectively discernable manifestation of God's presence. As another point of clarification, when I smell such a thing, I usually attribute it to the presence of Jesus Himself, not the Holy Spirit. This smell reminded me of a session in Washington, DC, about eighteen months ago during which Jesus manifested Himself with a cinnamon smell. Incredible healing miracles broke out in the room immediately afterward, including some people healed who had diabetes, autism, deafness, and metal knees. With that in mind, I stopped the teaching and told the group we would return to it, but I wanted to give Jesus the chance to interrupt the meeting as He wished. I prayed quietly for a moment and asked the Lord what that smell meant and what He wanted to do. I sensed He wanted to heal chemical imbalances and specifically to touch people with high and low thyroid conditions (all types).

Several people stood up for prayer, and the Holy Spirit began falling on them (or maybe Jesus Himself began touching them). However, just before all this, I had seen a large angel in the room, and based on prior experiences, I believe it was Raphael. Catholic and Orthodox teaching holds that he is one of the four archangels, specifically the one who carries healing. Raphael's wing brushed several people, and they were the ones who really "went off!" People began weeping, falling over, shaking, and the like. It is difficult to know exactly who was and was not healed because chemical imbalances don't lend themselves to immediate verification. However, several people testified that the symptoms of their chemical and thyroid conditions had all vanished.

Additionally, a few people were covered in gold dust. When I say "covered," I don't mean a few flakes. I mean *covered*. When the healing visitation ended, the gold seemed simply to fade away.

After about twenty-five minutes, we returned to the teaching, and things went "normally." We did have a move of the spirit of prophecy over the group, and some people got a first taste of what happens when multiple layers of prophecy come forth. That was very exciting as the Lord wove a "theme" through the many words and tongues (with interpretation) that came forth.

At two other times over the weekend, the Lord interrupted the teaching with scents. Once, He smelled like sandalwood. Another time He smelled like lemon, and that resulted in significant purging and cleansing from anger and bitterness, similar to what lemon juice does to the body when on a juice fast.

At Sunday's meeting, I also prayed for a teenage girl with a rare condition called LPE. I can't even remember what that stands for, but it is a serious condition that affects proteins in the body. The Lord touched her, but she won't get her next medical test for about two weeks. So we are encouraged but await definitive word.

December 19, 2014—
Los Angeles

The meetings we held recently in Playa del Carmen, south of Cancún, were strongly attended. Perhaps the most interesting and remarkable event was a deliverance that happened on the second night.

The woman we prayed for was clearly Mayan, and as the Lord moved on her, she began manifesting a powerful and unusual demon. She began making a noise that wasn't quite hissing but wasn't easy breathing either. She eventually ended up on the floor, and as we ministered to her, we couldn't figure out what allowed this demon to resist expulsion. She would begin wheezing and having extreme difficulty breathing, with no relief and no deliverance. Eventually, we told the spirits to name themselves. One called itself "Templo" (temple), while another sounded like "Ixtlan" and yet another something like "Ixipilanti." Through a word of knowledge, the Lord showed us a person locked in a vault or a chamber, and it gradually became clear that one of the woman's ancestors had been buried alive. We concluded that we were dealing with a familiar spirit (with other spirits under its dominion) that somehow was related to this awful event from long ago.

As we addressed the horror of live burial, the stronghold weakened. The spirit finally left with what sounded like a long, thready moan and a gust of wind (or something like that), then the woman coughed and became free. It was a very strong spirit. The whole experience was downright bizarre.

After searching the internet, we found that the spirit in question was associated with a semiautonomous region that never fully incorporated with the Mayan empire. It was home to an unusually bloodthirsty group that struck terror even into the hearts of the conquistadores, successfully resisting them. Its king was also a priest, and in addition to human sacrifice, the tribe often used live burial in its rituals.

So it is likely that we were dealing with some kind of regional ruling spirit. You can't make this stuff up!

PILLAR 5

Prayer

*And this is the confidence that we have toward him, that
if we ask anything according to his will he hears us. And
if we know that he hears us in whatever we ask, we
know that we have the requests that we have asked of him.*
—1 JOHN 5:14–15

A FEW YEARS AGO I attended a conference sponsored by the
Association of Vineyard Churches called "Doin' the Stuff
III." This was a conference intended to stir up the gifts and ministry of the Spirit among the Vineyard churches once again. There
were many good speakers, including US National Director Philip
Strout, Randy Clark, Robby Dawkins, and a pastor from Pennsylvania named Bruce Latshaw. Bruce gave one of the best messages on corporate prayer I have heard anywhere, and I have been
chewing on it ever since.

The Vineyard has many positive aspects as a movement, but
corporate prayer has always been a weak point. I remember "way
back in the day" how John Wimber tried repeatedly to implant a
passion for corporate prayer. He brought in Larry Lea, a pastor
from Rockwall, Texas, to teach on prayer. Later he brought in
Mike Bickle and Leonard Ravenhill. All of these were useful to
one degree or another, but group prayer never really caught on.
The Vineyard remained a largely prayerless movement, that is, in
the sense of corporate prayer.

It wasn't that prayer wasn't valued. It was. I myself was part
of a Saturday morning men's prayer group that saw amazing,

jaw-dropping answers to prayer. However, our group was never larger than fifteen, and typically only three to five of us met each week. The bigger problem as it pertained to prayer was that the early Vineyard leaders viewed themselves, in many cases, as "burned out Pharisees" who had come out from conventional religious backgrounds. Prayer meetings may have been part of their past, but because of the way they had been conducted, or perhaps due to the lack of specific answers, the practice was widely viewed as "religious" and therefore suspect. It is no surprise then that prayer efforts languished.

While I was in Costa Rica this past week, I got to thinking about corporate prayer—specifically about Acts 4:24, which reads, "They lifted their voices together to God." Two things stand out in my mind about this phrase: the first is that they lifted their voices, or "raised" their voices (to put it into modern parlance). In other words, they got loud. This isn't the kind of false excitement that is often "worked up" in many church circles, such as, "Come on, everyone, let's really praise the Lord! Let's give Jesus a shout and a clap offering!" Instead, this loudness comes from a genuine excitement that wells up from the depths of the soul. It usually involves a growing sense of a challenge soon to be overcome and celebrated. If you have ever been at a sporting event where a play suddenly excites the crowd or at a concert where the band begins a favorite song, you know the effect. People come right up out of their seats, shouting, screaming, chanting, raising their hands (often with their fingers making a "V" sign for victory), exploding with enthusiasm. That is the kind of dynamic that Luke is describing in this passage.

Yet this is not typical in most churches, including most Renewed or Fourth Wave/River Stream churches. Even if believers have gathered in the same room for a prayer meeting, prayer is inwardly focused, dialed down, and detached—reflecting Western individualism. Spoken prayers seem pained. Prayers spoken in unison are muted and sheepish, like a corporate board meeting where nobody dares to raise his or her voice (volume is the cardinal sin in formal or proper settings). No one dares to pray different prayers simultaneously (speaking over another is another cardinal sin in formal or proper settings). While I am not advocating for poor manners, this lack of engagement is a lost opportunity with unfortunate consequences. There is little expectation, and the body language, tone of voice, and energy level in the room betray boredom, a lack of enthusiasm, an uncertain faith. Nothing much comes out of those prayer meetings, and people generally loathe them, attending (if they do) out of guilt or a sense of duty.

We are missing out on the dynamic power that comes when voices are lifted together. Soldiers who are about to go into battle have known about this type of power for centuries, and in fact this dynamic is a key aspect of finding breakthrough in spiritual warfare. Let me repeat, I am *not* talking about a manufactured enthusiasm but rather one that arises from a deep, abiding confidence in God. It is a confidence that if we pray, and He hears us, then we *know* that we have what we ask for (1 John 5:14–15; note that John was at the prayer meeting in Acts 4:24, and it is likely that he learned this truth in just such prayer settings). That "knowing" of which John speaks is powerful; it breeds confident praying and a belief that our prayers can move heaven and earth. Such confidence tends to spill over into (gasp!) volume, excitement, and a sense of the imminent release of God's kingdom power. (See Acts 4:29–31.)

The second, other noteworthy aspect of Acts 4:24 is the word "together." The Greek word *homothumadon* is "a compound of two words meaning 'to rush along' and 'in unison.' The image is almost musical; a number of notes are sounded which, while different, harmonize in pitch and tone."[1] This unique word occurs twelve times in the New Testament, ten of them in the Book of Acts. If you have ever participated in a prayer meeting where this dynamic is in operation, you are familiar with the effect. If you haven't, mere descriptions won't sufficiently convey its power. It is like being in the midst of a vast symphony playing a fugue in which certain refrains recur, rising and falling. The instruments are tuned together, and an underlying, unifying theme emerges, to which the music returns continually, yet at various points it branches out and explores other themes. It is melodious yet woven into a rich, intricate complexity. Nevertheless, as the prayer rises, all present feel as though they are caught up in a whole that is greater than the sum of its parts. It is like being swept along by a current that is powerful, unyielding, irresistible. Or it is like a furnace whose various flames ascend together, mingling their heat into a hotter and hotter flame that ultimately can melt any metal known to man. Nothing can withstand this kind of prayer.

The unison that is presupposed in *homothumadon* is not the artificial unity that many have known whether in the church or outside of it. It cannot be commanded from an overarching authority. Nor is it the suppression of individual wills to create a humanly imposed unity. It is rather an enlivening of the soul through which people come together voluntarily with a common understanding and a common purpose or vision. It is what David spoke of:

> Behold, how good and pleasant it is when brothers dwell in unity! It is like the precious oil on the head, running down on the beard, on the beard of Aaron, running down on the collar of his robes! It is like the dew of Hermon, which falls on the mountains of Zion! For there the LORD has commanded the blessing, life forevermore.
>
> —PSALM 133

These two ideas combined—"voices lifted together in unity"—convey passion, and there is great power in passion. But passion (along with its frequent companion, emotion) puts some people off because in middle- and especially upper-class societies, open displays of emotion are frowned upon. The only places they might be tolerated are at weddings, births, and funerals (though not usually even at funerals, as mourners are expected to sit quietly, dabbing the corners of their eyes with a handkerchief). Consequently our social conventions may be one of the biggest obstacles to answered prayer. When our prayers go unanswered, our faith plummets. After a while, we lose heart and interest; just as nobody wants to follow a passionless leader, nobody wants to pray passionless (and consequently answerless) prayers.

I think it is time that we unplug the wells in our praying, rediscovering the power of passionate, unified prayer. It may not be the social norm, but it is biblical. If we can get comfortable with that fact, we may see the release of many things that we have all longed for.

How about it? Why not find one or two friends this week with whom you can connect in this kind of prayer—whether in person, over the phone, or on Skype/FaceTime? I believe that if we will do this, God will meet our passion and our unity by tearing open the heavens—in our lives, in our families, in our ministries, in our communities, in our nations.

"Ask of me, and I will make the nations your heritage" (Ps. 2:8).

February 19, 2015— Perth, Western Australia

I woke to the news that John Paul Jackson died overnight. I had seen a post about his approaching death before I went to bed and had prayed yet again for him to be healed as I have at different times throughout his ordeal. The Scripture that comes to mind is 2 Kings 13:14: "Now when Elisha had fallen sick with the illness of which he was to die, Joash king of Israel went down to him and wept before him, crying, 'My father, my father! The chariots of Israel and its horsemen!'" John Paul's battle was extended, and many mistakenly believed that when the cancer in his leg was found to be encapsulated, the battle was over. He did return to some of his normal activities for several months, but various complications arose. A great prophet has left us, but the last chapter is not yet written.

Somehow in my lifetime I have been graced to have relationships with several great men of God, each in a different way. These include John Wimber, Bob Jones, John Paul Jackson, Lonnie Frisbee, and some others who are still with us. John Wimber's influence in the kingdom is arguably greater in death than it was in life. "And through his faith, though he died, he still speaks" (Heb. 11:4). John Paul's legacy may be similar, although such matters take time—often years—to play out fully. We who are left must honor the legacy of those whom we love and admire by faithfully living out their teachings. Though their powerful ministries may have spurred us on, we cannot let up once they are gone. Just because the cat is away does not mean the mice can play. Instead we must go forth together and honor their vision of the city whose architect and builder is God Himself. This could apply to all of them, but today I am specifically thinking of John Paul.

Paul the apostle knew when the hour of his death was approaching, for he was to be executed by the Emperor Nero. Before his departure, he wrote to his disciple Timothy, "What you have heard from me in the presence of many witnesses entrust to faithful men, who will be able to teach others also" (2 Tim. 2:2). It is our job to entrust what we have learned to those who will *faithfully* and without deviation carry it forward. This is how we serve those who will come after us, most of whom we will never see or know. This is how we make sure that this faith we carry does not die out but endures for many generations.

Paul went on to give three illustrations of how this should work:

> Share in suffering as a good soldier of Christ Jesus. No soldier
> gets entangled in civilian pursuits, since his aim is to please

the one who enlisted him. An athlete is not crowned unless
he competes according to the rules. It is the hard-working
farmer who ought to have the first share of the crops.

—2 TIMOTHY 2:3–6

Paul's admonition is: (a) not to become discouraged by hardship or distracted and entangled in lower matters but to remain
faithful to the objective of pleasing the Lord; (b) to continue to
practice the faith as it should be practiced and not change the
rules (biblical teaching) to suit your tastes; and (c) to work hard,
with the promise that we will share in the fruit of our labors.

This is why we fight for healing so ardently and why we
actively seek to destroy the works of the evil one everywhere we
encounter them. Sickness and disease are *always* enemies, for
they are curses that come to us from the fall, and they reflect
the deep antipathy that Satan holds for the human race. They
have the power to kill us. They took my friend. They have taken
loved ones from all of us at one time or another. Even Jesus
tasted the bitterness of death for us, and when we grieve, He
grieves with us.

Hail and farewell, John Paul! Your suffering is now behind you.
You are still loved by many, and we thank you for all that you
taught us. We will see you when we get to heaven ourselves.

March 25, 2015—
San José, Costa Rica

It is day three, and the team has met with the local staff, the ministry team, a Monday group called "Fuego" (Fire), and a Tuesday
night group for people eighteen to forty years old called "Supernova."
In each meeting the Holy Spirit has moved differently—some
impartation but also healing and receiving of the gift of tongues.
Last night quite a few were on the floor weeping loudly.

Today we visited Funda Vida, a center that the church runs in a rough, poor area not far away. While we were there, a young man was shot and killed about one hundred meters away, and last week just outside the center a gun battle broke out between rival gangs, resulting in the killing of another youth. The church runs three such centers serving six hundred children in total. This particular one was once a drug house and onetime brothel with a caved-in roof. The pastor called it a "bunker." The church took over this old, dilapidated building and has completely renovated it with new floors, freshly painted walls, an education center, computer lab, and more. The children who come now express (of their own will) the desire to be teachers, engineers, and the like. The entire effort is based on the notion of the kingdom of God breaking into a rough, dangerous neighborhood. The long-term impact of such an effort is difficult to predict with certainty, but two-thirds of the crime in Costa Rica is drug-related and originates in neighborhoods like the one we visited. In this city alone, at least three thousand underage children are involved in the sex trade. It is difficult to overstate the emotional impact of Funda Vida. I found myself teary-eyed and weepy throughout our time there. [If you would like to learn more about the ministry of Funda Vida, visit www.fundavida.org.]

March 27, 2015—
San José

Last night's meeting was packed, with people standing at the back. I spoke on the kingdom of God, one of my standard "opening" messages for the first night of a conference.

At the conclusion, I called forward anyone who needed to believe in God again. About 75 percent of the people in the room filled the altar space. Then the Holy Spirit began moving. Some simply collapsed as knees buckled under the power of God, thereby eliminating any question of whether they had been pushed.

Others were crying and shaking, including a group of four men on the far left with interlocked arms. They fell together, despite their joined efforts to remain standing under the anointing.

After this had been going on for a while, healing began to break out. Several people were healed of injuries and pain in the C3/C4 area (called out by word of knowledge). Several were "healed in the glory" with nobody touching them, while others received their healings after "laying on of hands." There was also a word for stomach conditions, food allergies, and the like. Those are more difficult to measure immediately, so I don't know how to report on that word except to say that some seemed to get freed of "hitchhikers" as part of that prayer time.

The final healing I wish to report was of a man who came in with a cane. He'd had a stroke seven years earlier that left him paralyzed on the right side and unable to speak. He received about 50 percent healing; his curled hand uncurled, and he no longer needed his cane to walk. He also raised his right arm over his head (with minor assistance), whereas previously he could not lift it at all. He could also communicate clearly, without any slurring or other difficulties. That was a mostly satisfying end to the evening, although I always look for 100 percent healing. So while he was 50 percent healed, I was 50 percent disappointed, even in the midst of great thankfulness for the Lord's goodness. He's coming back tonight, so perhaps we will see him fully healed this evening. [He did get healed!]

March 31, 2015—
Los Angeles

I returned home last night, traveling through Houston to get here. The time in Costa Rica was fun, although we did have some "unusual" experiences. On Saturday morning, I was awakened to gunfire just outside my window—six shots in three pairs. The house where we were staying, while quite nice and very middle class, was, in fact, *directly* across the street from a typical Central/ South American barrio (shanty town). When I say directly across the street, I mean *literally*, perhaps ten to twelve meters away. Our hosts pastor a church in that community, and they wanted to be close to it. When I mentioned the gunfire over breakfast, they said the shots were likely fired from just outside our gate as people in the community often like to shoot from the fence that surrounds the house, over the ravine toward the barrio. However, they were unconcerned, saying it was just the tail end of the celebration we had all heard throughout the night. If it had been a killing, there would have been sirens.

Our last days in San José were marked by increasing power and visitation, although it did not come easily. We battled in prayer to get to that point, as did our intercessors. All of the team were on top of their game on this trip, with great unity and love, perseverance, and maturity despite nonstop ministry. The spirit of prophecy was moving consistently in our team also and with astounding accuracy, in many cases naming places, dates, names, and such.

One of the best parts was seeing a family brought back together after many years of brokenness. We also had several salvations on this trip, including some outside the services. Some of the team went to a local park one afternoon, just walking and not really looking for any evangelistic encounters. However, when they saw a boy with a broken arm, they prayed for him. He appeared to have been healed, but (naturally) they couldn't get the cast off to confirm it. Immediately thereafter, they led three people to Christ, including the boy. Another group visited the barrio across from where we were staying, and several people gathered to hear them share; they too gave their lives to Christ.

A few healings that stand out occurred too. One of them was a young woman with muscular dystrophy who had struggled with this condition for years. She received prayer and seemed improved but nevertheless returned the next day. When she received additional prayer, power surged through her body. She felt it, and so did I. Thereafter her left foot straightened out as did her hips. I felt led to ask her to walk with me in a marching fashion, lifting her legs high. The more we walked, the better she became. It is difficult to measure healing in these kinds of situations, so I hesitate to say she was X percent healed. But she clearly had a significant touch from God, and she was astounded to feel the power go through her. She left with a big smile and indicated she may share some of her story after she visits her doctor.

Another story involves a man in his thirties whose parents brought him for prayer. We agreed to meet on Sunday morning prior to the service because he was unable to sit through church, often acting up and sometimes becoming quite aggressive with people. He had suffered brain damage from an incorrect drug administered to his mother during his birth. The team met with him and his parents outside by their car and prayed for about fifteen to twenty minutes. The first seven to ten minutes were challenging as he kept acting up, hitting our hands away, crying out, spitting, and trying to walk away. However, we pressed on, quietly invoking the kingdom of God and asking for the power of the Holy Spirit to be released.

Around ten minutes into the prayer time, he seemed to calm down considerably. Peace came over him, and I got him to look into my eyes, which he did with a smile. I prayed for him several times with our gazes fixed upon each other. Later on, one of our Costa Rican team members received a text from his mother saying that her son had changed. He was talking normally, behaving normally, eating normally, not acting out, and not being aggressive. The tone of the message was of overwhelming joy, thanksgiving, and wonder that God would visit her son after such a long trial. I don't know what more to say; it was clear that *something* significant had happened.

I found Costa Rica to be a warm and comfortable place. God is stirring great faith in the hearts of the people there. Moreover, if the prophetic words are correct, there is a move of God underway that should become discernible in the next couple of years. Stay tuned as there will undoubtedly be many more stories coming out of that country in the near future.

April 18, 2015—
Taipei, Taiwan

I am very short on time this morning; I will write more later. Last night was a massive move of God with extensive deliverance and healing. I am not exaggerating when I say that golf ball-size tumors were simply vanishing and/or dematerializing in front of our eyes and under our hands! We had other dramatic healings, including of a few dozen sinus and respiratory conditions like deviated septa and unexplainable asthma.

One woman had made a deal in a temple when her father was sick, telling the idol that if her father would live ten more years, she would give up ten years of her life. He lived twenty-six more years, and she became deeply afflicted with unexplainable breathing problems, including noncancerous growths in her lungs that ranged from a few millimeters to over a centimeter. I had her renounce the vow to the idol, then I broke the curse (it took about three minutes of repetition to get things moving, so remember to persevere), at which point it all broke loose and came out with large amounts of sputum, bile, and tumors expelled from her lungs into a bag. She kept coughing and hacking for about thirty minutes, but when she left, she was radiant and able to breathe. Now *that* is what we are talking about!

Also people with arrhythmia had their hearts come back to

normal beating patterns, and some with deformed bones felt and heard them *snap* back into correct position and alignment. Things are rolling here in Taiwan, and one of the pastors said to me, "This must have been what Paul meant when he said that his gospel came with a demonstration of the Spirit and power. We need to stop arguing about words. Western theology is too busy trying to be respectable. It all makes sense when you see this."

Amen!

April 20, 2015— Danshui, Taiwan

Yesterday was an extremely long day. When we got to our room last night, I fell into bed and asleep in moments. The day started with a meeting in Taipei, where I addressed the topic of idolatry out of 1 Corinthians 10. I've personally never heard anyone preach on this, and it felt strange to be in a modern city speaking about such matters. However, the ministry time afterward showed its relevance. Nearly the entire church came forward, and people were finding lots of freedom: from idolatry they had engaged in, from ritual practices like the burning of incense and making drink and food offerings, as well as from ancestral sin.

Something I found on the last trip is being confirmed on this one—that this matter of ancestor worship is a big deal. Demons seek worship just as their master (Satan) does. They will masquerade as the dead (commonly called familiar spirits) to secure that worship, and when it is given, the victim is essentially immediately demonized. All manner of evil follows afterward. If you have ever "communed" with departed loved ones or "sensed their presence" and talked with them, you may have experienced the same kind of phenomena we have been seeing here. I could say much more, but that is all that time will permit at present. The ministry time yesterday morning could have gone for hours, but

I was pulled from there and taken to an afternoon meeting here in Danshui.

April 21, 2015—
Danshui

Yesterday I met with the Christian Women's Corps. While the group was small it was a very good meeting. The Christian Women's Corps was originally founded by a close associate of Chiang Kai-shek. I had not known that he and his family were Christian, but this probably explains in part the deep antipathy that Chiang Kai-shek and the Communist Chinese held for each other. In fact, the national museum houses his personal copy of the classic devotional *Streams in the Desert*, annotated and marked with his reflections and prayers over many years. Anyway, the group began back in 1949, and it has continued meeting, unbroken, ever since—that is, for more than sixty-five years. It consists of influential women from many walks of life; the woman who currently runs it is married to the man whose company manufactures *half* of all the jeans in the world. These pants are obviously rebranded as they make their way to store shelves, but if you are wearing a pair of jeans as you read this, there is a 50 percent chance that this family produced them.

I shared a message about walking with Christ and the ways of the Holy Spirit. The message seemed in many ways to be very new to these women, and they received the Word with great eagerness. Afterward, we had lunch and a ministry time, which involved much healing and even more prophecy.

My favorite story from the ministry time happened when I laid my hands on one of the women, and I immediately saw flowers. I paused, pondering what this might mean. I asked her if she liked flowers or was somehow involved in the flower business. (I could see flowers blooming everywhere—in particular, there were many yellow ones—and I could tell this meant "increase.") She looked at me with her eyes filling with tears and said, "Yes I am a florist. That is my business." I told her what I saw, and it turned out that yellow flowers are her favorite, although she obviously works with other colors too.

I told her I thought her business was about to grow and become more profitable, perhaps due to new customers or cheaper supplies of flowers. She told me that just that morning she had been asking the Lord for help with the business, that it would grow and prosper not only to support her and her family's needs but also to help finance the kingdom of God. God didn't take long to answer that woman's prayer. I am always amazed at how intimate and tender the Lord is with His people.

Today we will visit the new foundations of a church in Danshui, and tomorrow we will hold a miniconference. I am finding that the underlay of both Buddhism and even more importantly of Taoism is something that needs to be addressed. Similar to the "insider" movement in Islam that seeks to blend Christian teaching with Islam, a movement underway in Taiwan and China seeks to merge the teachings of the Buddha and the Tao with Christianity, resulting in a strange syncretism that hinders the spread of the Word of God—essentially, it enervates it completely. Based on the amount of deliverance we've seen over these two religions, I think it is clear where the Lord stands on this topic. Many of the believers are eager to learn more; nevertheless, the topic also has the potential to be a bit sensitive and even controversial.

April 23, 2015—
Taiwan High Speed Rail, Taipei to Tainan

We finished up in Danshui last night to a significant move of the Spirit. In the afternoon session, I taught on the transcendence of God and the immanence of the kingdom. Then I called the ministry team forward for impartation before turning them loose on the room. Most of the team ended up flattened under the power of God, laughing, weeping, or in trances. So the Lord decided to minister to the room Himself. Many (actually most) in the crowd had the power of God fall on them unexpectedly, and not a few simply fell out of their chairs and slid to the floor. I left after about thirty minutes to attend some prayer appointments, but I could hear from the sound in the room that, if anything, the intensity only kept increasing.

At night, I taught "Lessons for Kingdom Breakout." The healing time that followed was remarkable. My favorite story involves a woman who flew from Canada to Taiwan so that her daughter could receive prayer for fibromyalgia and chronic fatigue syndrome (CFS). The daughter was a weak, discouraged believer, and her mother was not a believer at all. The mother had told God she would give her life to Christ if He would heal her daughter. I'm not a big fan of such "bargains," but she had prayed this way before they ever walked into the meeting. Well, Jesus healed the daughter, and the woman gave her life to Christ, receiving baptism on the spot—pretty good for a night's work.

Healing these two particular diseases often involves releasing trauma in the body. Most commonly, although not universally, the trauma arises from verbal abuse/berating, often from one parent or the other. Such was the case last night. Once we addressed the verbal abuse and cleared the trauma from the body, the fibromyalgia was healed in a matter of a few minutes. The CFS took about thirty minutes longer. However, after prayer and some "floor time," the daughter walked around the church, and her strength continued to increase the more she walked. Somewhere in that time span, Jesus fixed her gait, so she could walk with a normal stride.

I came away from this portion of my time here with a unique picture from today's lunch. We were eating in a nice but modest

Taiwanese restaurant. I always enjoy the food here, so I was happily eating everything. As I put this piece of food on my plate, I asked my host what it was, as it looked like liver. (Many dislike liver, but I learned to like it as a child, even though I seldom eat it anymore.) When they told me it was pig's blood, I declined to eat it. Eating blood is far more common than most people realize and occurs in many cultures of the world. But eating blood in any form is explicitly forbidden in both the Old and New Testaments. We often drive out spirits that have entered through the eating of blood. I know this will offend and anger some readers, but I have Scripture and experience to back up what I am writing. Knowing this is a delicacy here in Taiwan explains why we have run into so many demons tied to the eating of blood. My experience is that ministering in a culture where the eating of blood is less common results in fewer expulsions of that type. As with many things in life, context matters.

April 27, 2015—
Taipei

I'm at the Taipei airport, preparing to head back to Los Angeles. The trip to Tainan was successful but a lot of hard work. *Every* person in the church came for a prayer appointment, and trust me when I say that none were easy cases. On Sunday, the first appointment occurred at 7:30 a.m., and we didn't finish until 3:45 p.m., with me preaching the Sunday morning service in the middle. The only break was about thirty minutes for worship. Then we rushed to catch the train back to Taipei. These ministry trips are rewarding, but they are certainly not vacations.

On Friday night, a woman brought her twenty-two-year-old daughter for prayer. The daughter had been afflicted with obsessive-compulsive disorder (OCD) since age twelve. The behaviors included the usual fixations and compulsive activities: picking at her hair and skin, as well as—in this case—bulimia. She could not perform at work and had recently asked to take a leave of absence because she could not handle the pressure from her supervisor, who was "mean" to her. It took a while to sort through her story as we had to translate between English and Chinese, but it turned out that the OCD began when she was rejected by five school-mates at her junior high school. I don't think the extreme cruelty of teenage girls, their "cliques," and the resulting shunning/bul-lying need any explanation. She had been on the receiving end of this kind of treatment, and none of the friendships ever recovered. Additionally, her teacher mocked her for her inability to perform her schoolwork and humiliated her in front of the class.

I took her through healing prayer over the rejection by her friends. During this time, she saw Jesus standing beside a weeping girl. She also heard Jesus tell her that the Lord is a shield, and she saw a shield given to her, large enough to hide her entire body. Next we drove out spirits of depression, rejection, and OCD (in that order). A manifestation of heat came over her stomach and chest, and the spirits came out with a long, thin moan—low in volume but unmistakable. That moan lasted nearly two min-utes, and she never took a breath. I don't know how that works physiologically.

After this, she said she still felt something in her chest. We paused to listen to the Holy Spirit, then I called out a spirit of bulimia, then suicide, and finally death. Unlike the first three spirits, these three left with loud screams and violent shaking. The final manifestation was of menthol or mint (like Vicks VapoRub) over her chest. This is quite common in the aftermath of deliv-erance, and it seems to be a sign of cleansing and sanctification. Then we prayed for the infilling of the Holy Spirit. She broke down in her mother's arms crying, saying repeatedly (in Chinese), "It's gone! It's gone! It's gone!" Jesus is Lord over OCD.

Friday's prayer time also featured the healing of two partially blind women, both of whom afterward could clearly see the time on the clock at the back of the church as well as the Chinese characters on the walls. Additionally, the mother of the young woman I just described was healed of a paralyzed shoulder. As she was receiving prayer, she said, "I would be happy not to be healed if God would just heal my daughter." She got both! God is good and generous.

On Saturday night, I preached on power and authority in the kingdom of God, then I asked who would like to operate in greater authority and receive the power. As people were standing, I said somewhat loudly, "God, give us a new Pentecost!" The presence and power that descended was something to behold. Seldom have I seen an entire room consumed like that: *Every single person* was under the power of the Spirit, shaking, sweating, crying, falling, and speaking *loudly* in tongues! Afterward, the pastor said he thought he had been transported back to the first century. Nobody there had ever seen or experienced anything like it before. It was a God moment, to be sure.

My biggest disappointment with the weekend was that one of the founding elders—a man in a wheelchair who had been injured in a motorcycle accident three years ago—was not healed despite two extended prayer sessions. He said he was slightly better, but I honestly could not see any difference. I think he was just being polite. He is the first paralytic or disabled person in a while who has not received healing. I need to go back and pray through that some more. It feels (rightly or wrongly) as though something has shifted, and in a way I don't like.

This is my final report from this year's visit to Taiwan. When I return next year, we will have a major conference that will involve several churches from around the nation. I love ministering in this country because it just feels so...biblical. There are hungry people, multiple gods as in the first century, demons to drive out, sick people to heal, and a largely unevangelized nation to reach.

The kingdom of God is advancing in Taiwan, and I think the Taiwanese churches are getting fired up enough to go after the whole of northern Asia. Can anyone say, "Regional outpouring"?

May 25, 2015—
Adelaide, South Australia

I returned from Whyalla yesterday, flying in on a Rex turbo-prop ("Rex" is short for "Regional Express" but is also Latin for "king" if you like prophetic symbols). The time in Whyalla was quieter than in prior years. However, people were certainly touched with both healing and impartation. In one session several severely injured or mobility-impaired shoulders were healed, and in another, the spirit of prophecy was moving in such a way that most people who came forward got words that seemed to hit the mark. In another session, a pastor went home freed from several memories that had plagued his personal life for many years (I am being deliberately discreet about the details).

There was also a woman who was significantly healed (but to be clear, not yet fully healed) in her eye. Several years before, she'd had a melanoma removed from the retina through the implantation of a radioactive patch in the back of her eye. A week later, they cut the eyeball open again to extract the patch. Her life was spared, but she never regained her peripheral vision. Oddly enough, getting to the degree of restoration she received entailed driving out a generational spirit of divination that came from her grandfather's water divining using "dowsing rods." She remembered his doing this, but she was unaware of the dangers of such activity. That he had done this was revealed through a word of knowledge. She wept as she realized that this had come through her Christian heritage. This woman's story highlights the grave danger of syncretism, even within the church community of a country with a "Christian heritage." It also shows how often lingering diseases and illnesses may have hidden roots that can only be uncovered by waiting on the Lord.

My topic in Whyalla was "Continuous Revival," and in debriefing with our host afterward, she said she thought the teaching challenged the status quo deeply, so perhaps people were more reflective than usual. Additionally, several of the elders were musing about how long the next elders' meeting might go as they sorted through all we had presented and discussed. Because of the location, some of the people (including some pastors) had driven considerable distances to participate. We were, after all, on the edge of the outback. I wonder what the impact will be as they carry away the messages and impartation to their home turfs. Only time will tell.

Finally, while in Whyalla, I had a strong sense that the Holy Spirit wants to start moving in the northwest of the state of South Australia. If one looks at a map, this area appears larger than Southern New England (in the United States) but has few roads. As I was considering this, someone told me that the region is a large Aboriginal homeland. This excited me because several words have stated that the move of the Holy Spirit in Australia will include all two hundred fifty Aboriginal tribes and not just WASP Australians from the UK and Scandinavia. So that was encouraging, but as with all such matters, I found myself asking how to follow it up or how to implement it.

Upon returning to Adelaide, I went directly to Southland Vineyard. Within the hour, I was speaking on the topic of the new orthodoxy, which entails the Word of God and the Spirit of God moving together in power. This is in distinction to the old orthodoxies, the one in which church tradition stands beside Scripture in value (in Mark 7:13, Jesus had warned that the traditions of men can invalidate the Word of God) and the other in which Scripture alone is sufficient. I know this was a touchpoint of the Reformation, and I don't mean in any way to undercut the authority of the Bible. However, Jesus said in speaking to the Sadducees that they erred because they understood neither the Scriptures nor the power of God. Clearly He thought *both* were necessary, so I tried to elaborate on that idea.

I had come to the meeting with a strong sense that the Lord wanted to move powerfully in healing and deliverance. We had a great ministry time that went late, with the entire prayer team joining in. A *lot* of people were healed of all kinds of things, including some longstanding conditions that had not responded to prayer, medication, or surgery.

In addition, a group of young Iranian men who are new converts came from a nearby church. They waited until late in the evening before asking to receive prayer for the baptism in the Holy Spirit. When we started praying, the Spirit's power fell like a bomb! I would have taken a short video, but I had my phone turned off rather than in flight mode as I usually do when speaking. I figured by the time the phone had finished booting up, the fun would be over, so I didn't try. Anyway, these seven men hit the floor crying, shaking, laughing, speaking in tongues—it looked like Pentecost, which it was for them. Their responsiveness to the Holy Spirit reminded me that their culture is closer to that of the original disciples who were present at the first Pentecost, and possibly, their receptivity and expressiveness reflected that. Said another way, maybe we don't see people being filled with the Holy Spirit like that in white Western society because we simply cannot allow ourselves the freedom to experience God like that or to be that expressive. (Or maybe, like the first disciples, God was equipping them to be able to face great persecution.) In any case, it was glorious and powerful.

May 28, 2015—
Melbourne, Australia

My last two days in Adelaide were extremely busy and included a luncheon meeting with a group of mostly Baptist pastors as well as two meetings at a Baptist church. I found the pastors hungry, full of good questions, and ready to see the Lord bless their denomination. As for the evening meetings, the Holy Spirit fell in the room the first night, with every person but one receiving either a new tongue or the gift of tongues. The one exception went home to seek the Lord about this and apparently found what he was seeking.

The second night the Lord healed three people in front of the room: two with spinal conditions that warped or bent their spines and one with plantar fasciitis. As that was finishing, the Holy Spirit came upon a woman, who fell into a prophetic ecstasy while speaking in tongues. Once that tongue was interpreted, the ministry time broke out more widely, resulting in a few people finding deliverance. That prophecy was literally a catalyst to a breakout of the kingdom of God. All in all, it was a good two days.

After Adelaide, I flew here to Melbourne for the final five days of this trip. First, I led a miniconference on "When the Spirit Comes." I could report many things, but my favorite time was when the Holy Spirit fell on a group of people gathered in a circle in classic daisy chain fashion at the front. For those unfamiliar with this term, this is something Lonnie Frisbee used to do— taking people who were in some way under the power of the Spirit and joining them with others so everyone in the "chain" would come under the Spirit's power as well. This "contagion" worked as well in 2015 Melbourne as it did back in the 1970s and 1980s in Southern California.

Later in the week, I taught on "The Apostolic Church" at an Anglican church in Doncaster (still metropolitan Melbourne).

Subsequent sessions included teaching on apostolic doctrine and apostolic lifestyle, and concluded with apostolic impact. The most eye-opening ministry session occurred after the session on apostolic doctrine, when several people were delivered of spirits of false doctrine of various types; in some cases, this led to the healing of food allergies. Who knew that false teaching could be so dangerous or contagious?

[The old model of false teaching says that when people are deceived, they just have wrong ideas that need to be straightened out through more teaching. It is true that they need new teaching. However, we have seen repeatedly that there really are spirits behind false teaching that need to be evicted for people to get free not only of the teaching but in many cases of their diseases and afflictions too. (See 1 Timothy 4:1–2.)]

Something palpable was brewing throughout this trip to Australia. It is a mixture of unity across churches, expectation for God to move, and a sense of mobilization among the people. This seems to be very broad, and it incorporates many streams and movements. I came home very encouraged that the river is rising.

June 7, 2015—
Boston

This weekend's conference on the apostolic church concluded with a morning service. A noteworthy thing that happened was watching the Holy Spirit fall on people as they recited the Apostle's Creed. I know this is viewed by many as boring liturgy, but it attracted the power of the Spirit, as it also did last weekend in Melbourne. Some of those in attendance were delivered of spirits from prior involvement in heretical or suborthodox movements.

Additionally, one woman gave her life to Christ and was "born again in power," falling to the ground under the power of the Spirit and speaking in tongues as she was birthed into the kingdom of God. I love it when this happens, and the message wasn't even evangelistic! This morning, many people came forward during the altar call to repent of things that may have been eating away at their Christian vitality. There were many tears down at the altar as well as actual sobbing. All of this was a different set of manifestations of the Spirit than healing and deliverance (for the most part), but it was unquestionable that the Holy Spirit was present and backed the teaching all the same.

Tonight I gave a simple message about healing, then it all began. Many more healings occurred tonight than I could keep track of. Also, we saw a fair amount of deliverance. One item I ran into tonight (and have been running into a lot recently) is Rosicrucianism. At first blush this appears to be a less common form of Freemasonry, but it is more insidious than that. It includes elements of soul travel/astral transport, divination, and the incorporation of Eastern gods from Hinduism as well as something called "The Christ" that is not what it appears. Rather, it is an antichrist spirit that masquerades as Christian; it denies Jesus' bodily resurrection and that Christ is the only way of salvation. If you happen to be ministering to someone who is a Rosicrucian or who comes from such a family, be on the lookout for these unique spiritual aspects of this very ancient cult.

New England has historically been a challenging place for Christian ministry. It seems that something is shifting here, not unlike what I sensed in Australia last week. I pray that we are ready and that the signs of the Spirit, including repentance, salvation, healing, and deliverance that have been going on this weekend, are harbingers of things soon to come.

June 16, 2015—
Los Angeles

This past weekend in Woodbridge, Virginia, was packed full of meetings, prayer appointments, and not much sleep. Much of what went on in Woodbridge was very private and personal, so I can't go into details about most of the ministry sessions. However, here are some things that are on my mind about ministry to people with sexual issues.

1. *The Hebrew definition of* nakedness *(as in "uncover the nakedness" of a person) is much more inclusive than modern thinking.* If the clothes come off, or if a hand or other body part touches someone's body even through the clothes (or under them), then biblically speaking a "sex act" has occurred. Think about that as a measuring line of why so many people feel defiled, dirty, or indifferent toward sex. What was created to be healthy and beautiful to unite two married people of the opposite sex has been sullied in the lives of most people. The thief really does come to steal, kill, and destroy.

2. *Freedom from that sense of dirtiness and indifference is possible.* Jesus delights in setting people like this free. Think of the story of Mary and the spikenard (John 12:3–8; Matt. 26:12) or the woman caught in adultery (John 8:3–11). Jesus was not repulsed by their sin, but neither did He endorse it. If He had endorsed it, they would not have been able to get free. We do people no favors by somehow validating their past.

3. In addition to what I just mentioned, *when people have been sexually molested, assaulted, or raped, they often have very confused feelings.* This is particularly true when they have been assaulted by a same-sex person and even more so when the assailant is also a family member (not just immediate family either—the Bible has a wider view of incest than just brothers and sisters or mother and father, as we see in Leviticus 18). In that case, there is now

both a homosexual issue and an incestuous one. Often people say nothing but go for years wondering and fearing that they are somehow homosexual, and they frequently feel great shame and guilt over these conflicted feelings. Telling them to explore the feelings or that they are normal *also* does them no favors. This is what our society is busy doing right now. Instead, telling them that this is not who they are and that Jesus can take away all that shame and guilt, then letting the Holy Spirit genuinely cleanse them, is the pathway to freedom.

When I talk about the power of the Holy Spirit, I don't mean some vague religious influence or sensibility. I am talking about the dynamic power of the third Person of the Godhead loosed to take away the damage of sexual assault to the mind, to the emotions, and to the human spirit. I am talking about the active power of cleansing and the power of God's own holiness to remake the human soul in the image that God intended. This is not something the world understands.

> And I will ask the Father, and he will give you another Helper, to be with you forever, even the Spirit of truth, *whom the world cannot receive, because it neither sees him nor knows him.* You know him, for he dwells with you and will be in you. I will not leave you [desolate] as orphans; I will come to you.
>
> —JOHN 14:16–18, EMPHASIS ADDED

Most churches don't understand this either, and it is one of the reasons (not the only one) that the church has largely rolled over and played dead on this issue. This kind of freedom is the hope we offer. Rather, the Lord Himself offers it through us—and it is the only solution to the rising tide of sexual perversion and iniquity that has been loosed upon the earth.

I say it is time to stand up and let people know there is a more excellent way.

June 22, 2015—
Los Angeles

I returned last night from a weekend trip to Orlando, Florida, where I taught a short course on deliverance at a church. I tried to keep the teaching short, but for those who haven't had much introduction to this subject, it can be challenging because *so* many questions pop up. Somehow we got through them all, and we managed to have some good ministry times.

In addition to the usual assortment of things, it was a bit surprising to run into several Nazi spirits (yes, you read that correctly) left over from the involvement of family members (usually two generations back) in the Nazi Party, Hitler Youth, and so on.[2] It is not well known that Nazism has strong occult roots, and some scholars (yes, scholars, not fanatical Christians) have argued that many of the atrocities committed by the Nazis were blood rituals to appease the occult entities that lie behind Nazism. Whatever you may believe about such claims, we ran into enough people with these spirits to cause me to shake my head in disbelief. Who would have thought that in the land of Disney World you would find such things?

Ministering to those afflicted by these spirits involves:

1. Having the person repent on behalf of their relatives for participating in occult-based activities as well as hate-based activities and any associated bloodshed.

2. Declaring openly that the person will not follow the teachings of the Nazi Party.

3. Pronouncing forgiveness over the person and their family for participating in Nazism.

4. Having the person tell any spirits associated with Nazism to leave, including the Nazi spirit, blood-lust, and witchcraft (plus *any others* the Holy Spirit shows you or the person).

5. You, as the prayer minister, telling the spirits to *come out*! (The capital letters and exclamation point do not indicate volume as much as they indicate authority.)

On a similar theme I am noticing that teaching on deliverance is suddenly becoming the "in" thing. Conferences, webinars, new books, etc., are popping up. A couple of years ago we started discussing how a wave of deliverance was coming globally. I think it has arrived. Get ready for more! I see this emphasis as the Lord's answer to the increasing wickedness on the earth for which there seems to be no answer. The Lord has the answers, but they may not always the be the ones people expect or want.

July 12, 2015— Baltimore to Los Angeles, 39,000 Feet

I finished up the weekend on the East Coast today with a visit to a church in Millersville, Maryland. All I can say is, "What a weekend!"

A factor that made this event so successful was the attendees' hunger. People were not only unashamed of getting free, they were also willing to testify about what God was doing in them in great detail! That proved that nobody was trying to put the Holy Spirit in the closet and that in addition to whatever freedom they received, they were free from shame. God is so good!

We had multiple deliverances of—well everything, from same-sex attraction and bisexuality to incubus and succubus spirits, Asian spirits that had entered through ancestor worship (that among other things caused food allergies and the inability to speak in tongues), to more commonly encountered conditions such as depression, suicidal ideation, and the like. In general, it was "open season." The enthusiasm was as high as anything I have seen in a long time.

We left on Saturday, later than planned (Is anyone surprised to hear that?) and traveled south from New Jersey to Maryland. When we got there, we met with some leaders, and the meeting went until about eleven p.m., when we simply couldn't go any longer. Today's church service was another one in which the Holy Spirit showed up with great power, and people were again getting free of deep and troubling problems. Additionally, a prophetess showed up at church and gave me a very lengthy and detailed word that I recorded, so I could digest it later. My initial take though was that this woman was on the money. That was a nice bonus to everything else. God is on the move in the Eastern United States, and I'm looking forward to returning in a month, when I will be in Oakton, Virginia.

July 22, 2015—
Geraldton, Western Australia

We leave this morning for a "morning tea" with some church leaders in Northampton. I expect this will be a small meeting due to the location and because it is a weekday morning. Notwithstanding, I am reminded that when Paul went to Ephesus he found "about" twelve men (Acts 19:7), and from that sprang the Ephesian revival.

It may seem farfetched, but the team and I are trying to put ourselves into position to be used by the Lord to trigger such moves of God. We haven't done it yet, but we have come close, and it "feels" like something is brewing in that respect as we head north today. This type of optimism is frequently required in itinerant ministry. While it is not quite the same thing as faith, it isn't unrelated to look for the good rather than focus merely on the difficulties and challenges that lie ahead. That doesn't mean you close your eyes to the difficulties, but rather choose (as an act of the will) to believe that the Lord will make a way even in the face of "headwinds." Isaiah expressed it this way:

> When you pass through the waters, I will be with you; and through the rivers, they shall not overwhelm you; when you walk through fire you shall not be burned, and the flame shall not consume you.
>
> —Isaiah 43:2

Challenges are inevitable; the outcome is not. With God all things are possible. So we are heading north with anticipation.

Last night here in Geraldton, the Lord moved on the crowd with great power as people responded to the call for renewed evangelism; I am eager to see the fruit that will come from it. Also, we had a woman apparently healed of double scoliosis. She relayed how she could feel movement in her back as we prayed and how all of the tingling and numbness in her toes left, one toe at a time. That healing took at least forty-five minutes to finish. Another woman appears to have been healed of an esophageal hernia.

Other healings occurred too, but these two were standouts in my mind. Of note, a woman who had come in a wheelchair, paralyzed for nearly fifteen years after a car accident, was *not* healed. She had a bright and cheerful spirit, but I felt deeply for her as she shared that at times she asked the Lord, "Why did this have to happen to me?" God is usually silent when we pose questions like that. She and a man in Taiwan are two paralyzed people who have not been healed of this type of condition this year, and I'm concerned. Last year and in 2013 the team was on a run with all kinds of maladies like this. This year has seen less success (so far).

The kingdom of God is at hand and is advancing to the

northwest of Australia! May the Lord give us the increase of His kingdom.

July 23, 2015—
Shark Bay, Western Australia

This is a small town sitting astride an inlet of the Indian Ocean. It is literally at the end of the road, nearly four hours north of Geraldton. That puts it almost as far north of Perth as Portland, Oregon, is from Los Angeles. Shark Bay was first settled five generations ago, and many descendants of the original convicts and settlers still live here. It might be difficult for those who live in urban or suburban areas to believe this, but there is just one main street with a couple of motels and bars, a few restaurants, a grocery store and a petrol station, an Anglican church, and Shark Bay Christian Fellowship, which hosted us. The pastor was driven out of the Anglican church many years ago after one of the shire council members conspired with the bishop to shut down a citywide revival. Five hundred souls call this town home, and a meaningful percentage of them (representing eight nations) "rocked up" for last night's meeting—this included "nearby" residents and Aboriginals, some of whom traveled more than two hundred thirty-five miles to attend.

I had gone for a walk after we arrived in town, and when I passed the fish-cleaning station along the foreshore, I knew I should scrap my healing message for a different one about long journeys. Nobody gets to a town like Shark Bay accidentally. A few may have come to return to their roots, but most are running away, seeking to disappear. They have literally hit the end of the road. So I talked about how God pursues people to the ends of the earth. Abraham in Haran, Elijah at Horeb, Jonah bound for Tarshish, and Peter at the Sea of Tiberias are all examples. David said it this way, "If I take the wings of the morning and dwell in the uttermost parts of the sea, even there your hand shall lead me, and your right hand shall hold me" (Ps. 139:9–10).

The denizens of Shark Bay realized that the Lord was after them last night; I saw His presence in a column of silver glitter at the opening prayer. One group of unsaved Aboriginal women had journeyed more than three hours to come, seeking healing. They found healing of deafness, freedom from arthritis, deliverance from smoking, and more. They came to realize that their hearts and their ways were far from God. They returned home and destroyed their idols, breaking their Buddhas(!), and turning to the living, true God. They sent word overnight that they had been visited and found. A woman who had come from Perth(!), more than nine hours south of here, and who works for the Roman Catholic Church also got healed, along with her husband. Laborers from the Philippines received prophetic words with tears.

Why go to places like Shark Bay?

> Jesus went throughout all the cities and villages, teaching... and proclaiming the gospel of the kingdom and healing every disease and every affliction.
>
> —Matthew 9:35

> And when it was day, he departed and went into a desolate place. And the people sought him and came to him, and would have kept him from leaving them, but he said to them, "I must preach the good news of the kingdom of God to the other towns as well; for I was sent for this purpose."
>
> —Luke 4:42–43

August 14, 2015—
Perth, Western Australia

I arrived here in the "City of Light" yesterday after the *long* trip from LA. It took fifteen and a half hours to cross the Pacific Ocean, then I had a layover at the Sydney airport that included a meeting with some Chinese leaders in the city, then another five-hour flight to Perth. Consequently, I was pretty flat when I arrived yesterday. Tonight at seven, the Christian Foundations of Healing and Deliverance conference begins.

I was in Washington, DC, last weekend, where I taught an entirely new conference called the Kingdom Is at Hand. We saw considerable freedom and healing come to the people, multiplied by the fact that we had a large enough team that everyone received ministry in some kind of reasonable interval. Several were healed of deafness, frozen or otherwise damaged shoulders and limbs, and internal-medicine kinds of issues. Notwithstanding the large team dynamic, Friday night went until 2 a.m. and Saturday went to 4 a.m. I wish I had the liberty to share some of the stories, but many of them were intensely personal and consequently unsuitable for discussion here.

The weekend before that I was in Sydney, where the meetings were full-on, flat-out—running early to late. My Sunday began at 8 a.m. and ended at 11:45 p.m. with only bathroom breaks between. The Lord touched many longstanding maladies and syndromes. Some were diseases, physical conditions, and emotional/mental conditions. Some people were freed completely, while others got started in the process after many long years of disappointment and waiting. I received a note from one of the staff, after this event, saying that many who had been coming to their healing rooms were finally healed the week following the conference, based on what we had discussed. The army is growing, and (in my best Reinhard Bonnke accent), "All Sydney shall be saved!"

Meanwhile, at least two people are in Perth this weekend to get more of what began two weeks ago in Sydney. We had a couple of sessions of "mass deliverance" two weeks ago, and while John Wimber wasn't a huge fan of this kind of ministry, he would occasionally do it. I remember once in Vancouver, British Columbia, where a large number of Canadian pastors got delivered en masse.

It seems that the Lord is highlighting the link between healing and deliverance these days; one might even say that in many cases healing comes through deliverance. There is a blurring of categories, even as the unique differences between healing and deliverance ministries are being delineated.

August 20, 2015—
Yallingup, Western Australia

It has been a busy last few days here in the southwest of Australia. The rain has been falling in abundance, and early spring is upon us.

This past weekend, I spoke at the Foundations of Christian Healing and Deliverance. It was a "redigging the wells" event to consolidate and elucidate what we covered in the deliverance conference in February. I find that coming to these concepts for the first time or two (or three) can require quite a shift of thinking. In addition, the ministry skills and the faith to carry them out sometimes elude people. Like sports, returning to the basics with additional elucidation can be a very helpful way to advance the skill set of believers. The event ended with a ministry session in the car park, which concluded at one thirty Sunday morning. We went home tired but excited at all the Lord did, including in the car park.

The next day I visited a Chinese church in Perth. I had been asked to teach a one-session seminar on healing and deliverance. That is a tall order, but I wrote a new "one session" message on the ministry of Jesus, and things really went well there. The power of God was profoundly and powerfully manifest, and many young adults were touched by God. "For unclean spirits, crying out with a loud voice, came out of many who had them" (Acts 8:7). Many were freed of evil spirits that came from a) eating blood; b) ancestor worship; and c) other gods (many came from families that were Buddhist, Taoist, or Confucian).

On Monday, we headed south to the tri-cities region of Bunbury, Busselton, and Dunsborough for three nights of meetings. On Tuesday morning we met with school chaplains who serve a region across Western Australia from Kalgoorlie to Esperance, from Albany to Augusta, and throughout the Busselton/Dunsborough area. It was remarkable to hear how the Lord is moving in the schools. There are many, many restrictions placed on these chaplains, but the Lord continues to bring students who ask about God, and little by little, kids/youth are being saved.

In Kalgoorlie, where prostitution is legal, open, and accessible (including "booths" that line the main street), a salacious sign was placed by a school crosswalk enticing people into a particular hotel that served as a large brothel. The chaplain raised the issue and said the sign needed to go. Nobody paid much attention, so she prayed that the Lord would remove the problem. A few days later, the hotel literally collapsed without warning into a pile of dust and bricks, taking with it the sign. The building had been a protected historic site, but the Lord had other ideas. Miraculously, nobody was injured or killed. I heard several stories of this type, although not all were as dramatic as this one. At the end of the session with the chaplains, the Lord moved among them with a very sure word of prophecy in operation.

Notwithstanding, much work remains to be done. A touch from the Spirit is important and necessary, but we need to ask the Lord for more chaplains, more mentors, and more open hearts. Just days before, the lead chaplain had received a call from a school principal in this region who said that he and his teachers are being overrun by the drug abuse, sexual excess, suicidal despair, and other problems among students. The man is an atheist, and his plaintive question to her was, "Where are the churches?" Indeed. Where are they? Why aren't they ministering alongside these chaplains and elsewhere?

The next day I met with regional pastors and leaders. The first night I was here, we had put on a white board a series of initiatives that the Lord seemed to be indicating He wanted to address during our time together. They included youth ministry, repentance (with a specific focus on unity), ministry to break fear, loose restriction, and releasing joy among God's people. I had received prior word that the leaders wanted to revisit these five emphases.

As it happened, we never did get to the planned agenda. Instead, the Spirit of God fell on the room in a manifestation of His burden for the youth of the region. Several of those present were reduced to tears as stories emerged from outreach initiatives the others knew nothing about; some stories involved kids who could not go home because it is unsafe, and more. It seemed that the Lord was calling the churches to band together to raise up youth centers, mentoring, and regional youth events like Youth Alive—overall, a remarkable meeting but entirely different than we expected. I love it when the Lord decides to take over and change the agenda (although I can easily see unity, fearlessness, and joy flowing out of obedience to the Spirit's leading regarding the youth). Of course now the real work begins of implementing all that the Lord spoke.

Things are stirring deeply and shifting in Western Australia, but there remains much work to be done. I see revival on the horizon, but it is still only the size of man's hand. Let's tuck in our cloaks, get to work, and run all the way to Jezreel, for there is a sound of heavy rain coming (1 Kings 18:41–46).

August 29, 2015— Kalgoorlie, Western Australia

This is a very unusual town, and I really like it here. The main street looks like a turn-of-the-century Victorian mining community, and interesting shops and eateries are scattered about. Kalgoorlie is the home of the Super Pit, then the largest open pit gold mine in the world. Gold has made the area wealthy; you can tell that it is not your typical small Aussie town. The area has a population of roughly thirty thousand people, but as the chairman of the church board said to me, "It punches above its weight."

I've just concluded the third meeting here, and each time things seem to become more clear and powerful. The local Church of Christ has thrown open the doors, and tonight we had representatives from nearly all eighteen churches in the city. Things are stirring in Kalgoorlie, and the hunger of the people is palpable. Tomorrow we finish up, and many are praying for a profound move of God. One of the things the Lord has been speaking to me here is, "The problem is usually not the problem." Not all that glitters is gold, and not all who wander are lost. When praying for people, cities, and nations, ask the Lord for the roots. Ask the Lord to reveal the things that burden Him. Follow those promptings because often what is needed to set people free is not what initially presents itself.

This town has a history of influencing matters far beyond itself, even at the national and international level. Representatives of many nations are here due to the international aspect of mining. Certainly, much more is going on than meets the eye, and it seems that the Lord may be giving us the keys to see Kalgoorlie break wide open. I am being invigorated by this visit, and if I see an angel tomorrow, I won't be surprised.

[I did see one. Actually I saw two. I saw one on the edge of the open pit of the mine and one in the church when I walked in. After those meetings were over, the pastor said to me, "I went to the John Wimber meetings in Perth many years ago. I have not seen meetings this powerful since then. I never thought I'd see it in my own town." So maybe the angel of the Lord was helping me.]

September 1. 2015— Lawang. Jawa. Indonesia

I arrived here yesterday afternoon after taking the overnight flight from Perth to Singapore and from there to Surabaya. During the weekend, I prayed with a young man who was powerfully touched by the Lord. His spiritual life had been on-again off-again for many years, but when we got to the root, he had an encounter with God unlike anything he had ever experienced previously, despite being from a Christian family. He wrote to me and said he had never felt God manifest power upon him like that; it was the most profound experience with God he has ever had. He said his life wouldn't be the same going forward, and he is determined to walk with Him from here on out. If you knew his history, you would understand how big of a statement this is, but due to the size of Kalgoorlie, I can't really say much more without divulging personal secrets and identifying the person. God is good, and He goes even to small, remote towns to seek and to save those who are lost.

September 3. 2015— Lawang. Jawa

The team is here for a leadership conference titled "Word, Spirit, Fellowship," with pastors and elders in attendance from churches throughout the Indonesian archipelago. This morning we had a healing move in which all but one person was healed. A follow-up is planned to see if we can sort out what the hindrance may be and pray it through—in this case, possibly a Western cultural bias. Tonight, the Spirit moved powerfully over the group as the elders committed themselves to the servant leadership model of Jesus.

Yesterday was interesting. In the morning I couldn't keep anything down. I had a fever, aches, and the like. This "flu" has been going around in Australia and Indonesia, and on the flight from Singapore a man was coughing and sniffing next to me the entire time. So when I began to get sick, I accepted my fate. After last night's teaching, the Lord moved in a massive deliverance from shame and failure for the elders and leaders, and while ministry was going on, my friend offered to pray for me. I thought, "This is ridiculous. Fevers are spirits, and this thing should go!" So I told him to go for it and to rebuke the fever like it was a spirit and tell it to leave. I also told it to leave, agreeing with him as he prayed. I coughed rather strongly (as you would in a coughing fit), felt a wave of nausea for a few moments, then it was gone! The fever left, my joints no longer ached, my stomach settled down, and I was able to eat dinner. Who knew? Attack and counterattack are real dynamics in spiritual warfare.

Tomorrow we will continue with teaching on the nature of true fellowship in the church and more teaching about the Word, on anointing, and operating in the anointing. We are seeking to raise the next generation of leaders and to "up the game" of the Indonesian church. Things are off to a good start.

September 4, 2015—
Lawang, Jawa

We had an exceptional morning today. After a stirring time of worship, I taught on the spirit of prophecy and how it should come with accompanying power, using Numbers 11, 1 Samuel 10:1–7 and 16:13–4, and Acts 2:1–4. Then the Holy Spirit fell like a bomb!

In the midst of it all something amazing happened that I haven't seen in a mass of people in several years. Supernatural fire began moving through the room, and over two hundred people were undone, completely "wrecked" in the Spirit. Substantial, palpable freedom was released. It was exhilarating, terrifying, and glorious. Then the spirit of prophecy began moving, and people were called out of their seats and given specific words. One man was struck to the ground under the Spirit (and I say struck rather than fell because of the force with which he went down). He received the Word and lay for some time, weeping.

We are going back for more this afternoon. More, Lord! *Maranatha!* Come, Lord Jesus!

Epilogue

A GENERATION AGO THE Charismatic world was thrilled and enthralled by the appearance of modern prophets, including Paul Cain, Bob Jones, John Paul Jackson, and James Goll. Paul Cain prophesied the coming of Joel's army, which was a metaphor based on Joel 2:3–9, a generation of Christians the Lord would use to work signs and wonders as part of a great evangelistic harvest near the end of the age.

Similarly, Bob Jones spoke of a coming "billion-soul harvest" in which a billion people from all over the earth would come to the Lord near the end of the age. These billion would be "fish cleaners" who would "clean the fish caught in the next big catch." This too was a prophetic metaphor for discipling and training the next wave of harvest, which he prophesied would be another three billion strong. These twin harvests were prophesied to precede the end of the present age, and as of this writing, they have not been fulfilled—although some would argue that the billion-soul harvest is now underway, principally in the non-Western world.

The things about which I have written are not common in the modern Western church today, although there are pockets or zones of visitation—places where they do happen. Sometimes they happen with reasonable regularity, while other times they are more sporadic. Where they are happening with the greatest overall frequency is in the two-thirds world described variously as the 10/40 Window, the majority world, and the new/next Christendom, to list a few. The Western church often views reports from this region skeptically or dismisses them altogether, usually based on the assumption that the medical documentation (where it exists) isn't up to Western reporting standards, the miracles are conflated with exaggerated claims by people who don't understand Western standards of reporting, or for other similar reasons. This is the very reason I have taken pains to point out in this book the times I wasn't sure of the ultimate disposition of the specific cases included. On the other hand, where the outcome is known and verified, I have also pointed that out.

Where does this leave us? Even if the events recounted herein aren't "normal" in the Western church, they are normal by the standards of Jesus and the apostles—provided the Bible is taken seriously. In many places it is not. The fact that signs and wonders may not be common, and that biblical testimonies of them are so widely ignored or discounted, highlights the tragic state of the Western church. Like the church of Ephesus, we have left our first love and lost the memory of whence we have fallen and we are no longer doing the works we did at first (Rev. 2:4–5). Such a widespread condition shows the need for a new reformation within the Western church.

The last great reformation recovered the authority of the written Word of God but generally without the power of the Holy Spirit. Additionally, much of the ground taken in the last great reformation has been lost in the twentieth and twenty-first centuries. The new reformation must feature both the Word and the Spirit. What might be the shape of such a reformation? First, at a minimum, it includes repentance from unbelief about the Word of God and the power of the Holy Spirit, along with repentance from dead works that may appear religious but fail to bear fruit that looks like the ministry of Jesus and the apostles. Second, it means moving away from commercializing the gospel and addressing the celebrity culture that has turned the faith into a "spectator sport" rather than a "participant sport." Third, it means embracing a lifestyle of the five *P's*. Fourth, it means a renewed emphasis on the Great Commission and discipleship.

Only if these things happen will the "billion-soul harvest" and the "three billion-soul harvest" that follows the billion-soul harvest occur.

Friends, we don't need to go to Sri Lanka or Indonesia or China to participate in the move of God. We just need to follow the four steps just described, reconnect deeply with the Lord, and become active participants in hastening His coming (2 Pet. 3:12), wherever we may be. The kingdom of God is not a place; it is the effective activity of God released in a specific place and time.

The kingdom of God is at hand, and it is advancing! What is your role in that advance?

APPENDIX A

Expectation

EXPECTATION IS THE best single definition of *active faith*. A roomful of expectation is a room where miracles will happen. The question is not, Will God do something? but, What will God do *today*?

My thoughts lead me back to 2011, when we all had a sense of anticipation. We were experiencing something that seemed bigger than ourselves, and we felt humbled that we were lucky enough to be a part of it. It reminded me of the words of Luke 3:15, "the people were in expectation...." The people of Luke's day were convinced that the Messiah—the Lord—was about to be revealed! In 2011, we similarly sensed that the Lord was about to reveal Himself in many new and surprising ways. With that expectation came a sense of awe. What would God do next? We invented an acronym, YCMTSU (you can't make this stuff up), because so many "coincidences" were happening each day, each clearly the finger of God and the confirmation of the Spirit we were living in.

Expectation is a concept that has gotten a bad rap in some church circles. In their honest desire not to see people hurt, some good-hearted leaders want to tamp down expectation. There may be a place for this, particularly when expectation is founded upon unscriptural footings or when wild promises that cannot be honored are made publicly. Nevertheless, for all of the possibility of error and abuse, expectation is something we should want in our midst. It is commanded in Scripture.

Expectation could be translated "eager waiting," as in Psalm

62:5: "My soul, wait thou only upon God; for my expectation is from him" (KJV). The NASB renders this same verse, "My soul, wait in silence for God alone, for my hope is from Him." We see here that expectation is tied to the theological grace of hope, which is saying a great deal because we are clearly told in Romans 5:5 that "hope does not disappoint because the love of God has been poured out within our hearts through the Holy Spirit who was given to us" (NASB). Paul picks up this same theme in Philippians 3:20, where he writes, "For our citizenship is in heaven, from which we also eagerly wait for a Savior, the Lord Jesus Christ" (NASB). Hope does not disappoint; therefore it points us to guaranteed outcomes. We see this again in Romans 8:19: "For the creation waits with eager longing ["anxious longing" in the NASB1995 and "earnest expectation" in the KJV] for the revealing of the sons of God." The common thread woven through these passages is that we are encouraged and even commanded to have that kind of eager, hopeful, earnest expectation for God to reveal Himself in acts of compassion, salvation, redemption, and deliverance.

Some want the focus of our expectation to be solely outward—to the end-time—but Psalm 62:5 is clearly looking for a present, current breakthrough from God. David looked to the Lord to resolve his trials and afflictions. If God were to rescue him one hundred, five hundred, or one thousand years later it would do him no good, and just so with us. Philippians 3:20 makes it clear that the eager waiting being commanded is the eager expectation of the Lord Jesus coming into the here and now to wrap up the ages. Meanwhile, the language of Romans 8:19 breathes a sense of "maybe the revealing of the sons [and daughters] of God could happen at any moment, perhaps even right *now!*" In fact, if anything could discourage us from having a present, eager sense of expectation, it would be the delay in the appearing (*parousia*) of Jesus Himself, for we are still waiting almost twenty centuries later! Yet nobody who is serious about the faith seeks to discourage Christians from living in eager expectation of the appearance of the Lord. Or do they?

There is something lighthearted and joyful, whimsical and musical, powerful yet disarming about those who genuinely live in hope. These are the ones who have a sense that Jesus really could come back *any* time. These are the ones who expect that until He does return, Jesus surely will and *should* accompany them as they go about their daily duties. These are the ones who have encounters with the unsaved at psychic fairs, in coffee shops, and—yes—even in churches. You can instantly tell the people who live this way from the ones who do not. People without hope are dour, plodding, trudging along in life, "just getting it done with the Lord, somehow." People with hope have an eager anticipation of quotidian miracles. It is a pretty clear litmus test. Expectation is the "combustible fuel" of faith.

In 2011, we sensed that God had come to visit us, and He did not intend to let us down. Prophecies were being fulfilled, miracles were happening, brothers and sisters were being reconciled, healing was breaking out everywhere, demons were being cast out, freedom was coming to those who lived in darkness and bondage, and all were captured by the love of the Father toward them. They were heady days, yes, but they were also "glory days," for the glory of God was upon us as a people.

The Lord has decided to throw a party, and against all odds, we are invited. He has checked the guest list, and it is called the Book of Life. If you are on the list, you are invited to the party—now in our present day. Of course, parties are only fun if you attend them. Sometimes people don't attend parties because they think they won't enjoy themselves. For them, I am reminded of the words of a preacher, who once said, "God spare us from the curse of low expectations."

APPENDIX B

Freemasonry

THROUGHOUT THIS BOOK I've mentioned setting people free from Freemasonry and why Freemasonry is a problem. Let me delve more deeply into that issue here.

Freemasonry dates back at least to the building of the great cathedrals of Europe in the eleventh and twelfth centuries. Some scholars believe it goes back all the way to the building of the pyramids. The cities of Washington, DC, and Canberra, Australia (to name only two), were laid out by the Freemasons. Freemasonry is extremely common in Western societies, but much of it is shrouded in mystery because it is a secret order and its followers are forbidden from discussing its beliefs and rituals with those who are uninitiated. Additionally, higher-ranking Masons are forbidden from discussing the rituals associated with their level(s) with lower-level Masons. Moreover, Westerners (who are routinely desensitized to spiritual matters) commonly assume it to be just another civic organization like the Rotary Club or the Kiwanis Club.

Nothing could be further from the truth.

Freemasonry is not Christianity, even though it may use Bibles or other Christian symbols. In fact, Freemasonry is found in Christian and non-Christian societies. Kemal Atatürk, the founder of modern Turkey (and a secularized Muslim), is one of its more famous non-Christian adherents. Freemasonry is syncretism, the mingling of Christianity with pagan rites and rituals. Among the more common branches of Freemasonry are Job's Daughters, the Order of the Eastern Star, the Scottish Rite, the Shriners, and the York Rite, but there are others. While Freemasonry is most commonly associated with men (i.e., fathers and grandfathers), it also can occur in women as there are specific groupings within Freemasonry for them (namely, Rainbow for Girls, Job's Daughters, and the Order of the Eastern Star). In general, its effects are transmitted either through personal participation or through direct lineal descent from a participant.

The ruling spirit over Freemasonry is named Jahbulon, which is itself an amalgamation of the names of three deities: Jah from the Hebrew God Yahweh, Bul from the Canaanite deity Baal, and On from the Egyptian god Osiris (the god of the underworld).[1] Freemasons first undergo an initiation ritual, then a series of other rituals as they rise within the order. They seek blessing through an oath of loyalty to Jahbulon and his subordinates, and they in turn pledge their "issue" (descendants) over to this entity and to the service of the Lodge. Curses accrue if any of the Freemason's "issue" should break from the Lodge. Due to these curses, disease often travels in families with Freemasons in them.

When praying with people to be freed from Freemasonry, here are the common steps. You are welcome to use the prayers verbatim, but it is the substance of the words, not the words themselves, that matters:

1. Ask the Holy Spirit to empower and oversee the prayer session: "Holy Spirit, we ask You to join us as we pray and to give us understanding and power. We welcome You to expose what lies hidden and to bring freedom."

2. Have the person repent on behalf of his or her ancestors for participating in Freemasonry: "Father, I ask you to forgive me and my ancestors [insert names and/or family relationship(s) here] for participating in Freemasonry. You alone are God, and

You alone deserve our allegiance. My family has violated the first commandment by swearing allegiance to a deity named Jahbulon who is not God, and I ask for forgiveness to come down over them and over me." The scriptural basis for this is found in the Book of Nehemiah, where he prayed for forgiveness on behalf of his ancestors (Ezra 9:7; Neh. 1:6–7; 9:16–10:39).

3. Have the person declare their allegiance to Jesus Christ: "I confess that I am a Christian and that my loyalties are solely to Jesus Christ as my Lord." Obviously if the person wasn't a Christian when you began the prayer session, then lead them to Christ at this step.

4. Have the person renounce the blessings and the curses along with the vows and covenants of the Masonic Lodge: "I now renounce the blessings of the Lodge and the curses of the Lodge. I no longer want its benefits, nor will I be bound by its curses. I also renounce the vows and covenants of the Lodge and will not honor them. I declare that I am under the blood of Jesus, and the power of these things was defeated by Him on the cross" (Col. 2:14–15).

5. Have the person renounce Jahbulon: "I hereby renounce the oath of loyalty taken by my ancestor(s) [insert name and/or family relationship(s) here] to Jahbulon. I forever separate myself from you, Jahbulon, and on the authority of Jesus Christ, I command you to release me and go! I will not serve you or the Lodge." I should

add that you should do this if you know someone in your direct line of descent (parents, grandparent, great-grandparent, and so forth—not so much aunts, uncles, cousins) to be involved for a fact; then we can go after it with confidence. If you suspect involvement by a direct ancestor but don't know for sure, ask the Lord. He will often reveal (perhaps not in the moment) whether it is in your family line.

6. You as the prayer minister now must command Jahbulon to leave: "Jahbulon, in Jesus' name, I command you to release your hold over [insert the person's name here] and *come out*! You are trespassing on God's property, and you must *go*! Leave now!" Note: The italicized words indicate the use of a forceful, commanding authority that the believer possesses in Christ. This authority is unrelated to voice volume, but it must be invoked.

7. Moreover many people believe that renunciation (step five) is sufficient to get free. Renunciation is a necessary first step, but it is not sufficient to cause demons to leave. Demons leave when they are driven out. They do not simply "drift away quietly." It may be helpful to think of renunciation as a choosing of sides before engaging in battle.

8. Press the attack and continue speaking to Jahbulon, commanding him to leave! For those who have not done much of this kind of ministry, it is common to hesitate or even to assume something didn't work if there is no immediate reaction. However, spirits will often lie quietly, hoping

the prayer minister(s) will break off the attack, thinking, "This isn't working. I'm just making this up." When the spirits begin to break and leave, it is common for the person to begin retching, coughing, sneezing, belching, shivering, shaking, and exhibiting similar manifestations. Having said that, occasionally the person will feel the spirit leave or lift, but you as the prayer minister will not have seen an overt manifestation. This isn't the norm, but I say this because we aren't chasing manifestations; we are chasing freedom for the person for whom we are praying.

9. Now check for spirits of death and infirmity. It is very common for these two spirits in particular to be present with Jahbulon (although there can also be others). Say, "If there are spirits of death or infirmity present, I command you to leave in the name of Jesus Christ! Come out now!" Again it is common for fairly obvious manifestations to be present as the spirits leave. Note that sometimes you will run into death and/or infirmity before dealing with Jahbulon. If so, drive them out first. The order in which these spirits leave is less important than that they do.

10. After Jahbulon, death, and infirmity have been driven out, pray against any spirits that may be tied specifically to the afflictions the person suffers from: "In the name of Jesus, spirit of fibromyalgia [or IBS or whatever], *come out!*" As noted, there will commonly be some kind of manifestation when you do this. After the spirit has left, pray for healing of the associated condition. Once

the spirit has been evicted it is usually easy to pray for healing of the condition. Note, however, that this does not necessarily mean it will be instantaneous. Take as long as necessary to get one condition healed before moving to the next. The pattern is: evict the demon(s), then pray for the healing until you have addressed all the conditions the person has.

These guidelines are exactly that—guidelines. If the Holy Spirit leads you in a different direction, and you are seeing results, then go with that. He will guide you into all truth. One of the greatest risks to ministry of the Spirit is when people become too formulaic and rigid in their approach. Be encouraged that God is more committed to the person's freedom than you or they are. "He who calls you is faithful; he will surely do it" (1 Thess. 5:24).

APPENDIX C

The Sixth P: Pedagogy

THROUGHOUT THIS BOOK I've presented the five *P*'s—the pillars that must be present to live a life of modern-day miracles. But there is a sixth *P*: sound teaching is the foundation upon which all the other *P*'s are resting. Unfortunately, there are some very unsound teachings currently running through the body of Christ.

Protestant theology, by its very name, was a "protest" to some admittedly bad abuses in the medieval church. We tend to idealize Protestant founders (speaking as a Protestant fellow traveler), but in fact, their theology was far from perfect, and their Christian practice varied between being better and worse than their theology. At times, they overreacted and other times they underreacted in ways that greatly distorted or even denied biblical truth. On some issues, they did both, compared to the teaching of Scripture.

A crucial problem with Protestantism early on was a misunderstanding of the person and work of the Spirit and, in particular, the nature of spiritual gifts. In general, most Protestant theologies denied them. Because one of the ways pastors and theologians are trained is to read the writings of the "great teachers," those denials have been propagated and reinforced for more than five hundred years.

In fact, a crucial part of the mission of Jesus was to give the Holy Spirit (who is more than an influence and more than an "it") to believers so that they might live as He did (1 John 4:17). Some would argue that the delivery of the gifts of the Spirit was central to the mission of Jesus. If you want to study this further, see the eleventh chapter of Jon Mark Ruthven's book *What's Wrong With Protestant Theology?*

Admittedly, part of the traditional Catholic and Protestant resistance to the idea of ongoing revelation to the laity is due to the danger of theological or practical excess. Sometimes "Charismatic craziness" goes to the point of contradicting Scripture. While God does speak to us through present revelation, such revelation must never contradict Scripture. That is one of the tests of true prophecy. Jesus said it best: "Heaven and earth will pass away, but my words will not pass away" (Matt. 24:35; cf. Matt. 5:17, "Do not think that I have come to abolish the Law or the Prophets.").

The comparison chart that follows lays out twenty-two points of disagreement between Catholic and Protestant theology (sometimes in their extremes and mostly without qualification), while not attempting to enumerate their biblically valid positions.[1] This choice of presentation is only meant to highlight how both might differ from "The Jesus Model."

The chart is not intended to criticize either Catholics or Protestants. It is, instead, a simple way of seeing the differences and similarities between the three positions and may help readers understand the basis of what has come to be known as Third/Fourth Wave Christianity. Catholic and Protestant theologies have much that is "right." Also the gifts of the Holy Spirit have been revived via Charismatic movements within several denominations. I present this synopsis to help you think about how your faith may differ from other Christian traditions and, most importantly, to offer a safeguard against falling into error or heresy.

Issue	Catholic Abuses	Protestant Reaction	Jesus' Model
1. Means of Salvation	Salvation by sale of indulgences to earn heaven; salvation by works	Salvation by grace alone; no works. Recite a prayer and you are in. It is a free gift. Nothing added.	Salvation begins with repentance and includes heaven along with gifts of healing and deliverance.
2. Benefits of Salvation	Salvation is escape from hell but may include purgatory.	Salvation is escape from hell, and it brings the promise of heaven.	Salvation is restoration from Satan's dominion via kingdom breakthrough by our "hearing" revelation, healing, power, and love.
3. Source of Authority	One's authority comes from miracles he does, which confirm his words are true (sainthood).	One's authority comes from Scripture proofs, especially the teaching/ didactic sections of the Bible.	One's authority comes from living out of the Father's initiative, without denying Scripture (John 5:19–20, 30).
4. Apostolic Ministry	The Pope is the "last apostle," and His authority and writings are infallible when spoken ex cathedra.	Apostles were the first and only ones to speak authoritatively to the church via their writings (the New Testament).	Apostles continue, as one of the "office gifts" and possibly one of the best gifts, expressed through being "sent out" to demonstrate the kingdom of God in power and love.
5. Knowing Truth	Truth = information: what the Pope and church tradition declare.	Truth = information from the doctrine with proof texts as formulated (doctrine of *sola scriptura*).	Truth comes by revelation of the Holy Spirit but is consistent with and does not contradict Scripture.

Issue	Catholic Abuses	Protestant Reaction	Jesus' Model
6. The Nature of Faith	I am to put my faith in the church's beliefs (assent to the creeds).	"The faith" is a statement of propositions (a creed) apparently supported by Scriptures.	Faith is a gift that comes by hearing a word of revelation ("assurance," according to Hebrews 11:1) that demands our obedience to God's direct "word" if we are to "live" (Matt. 4:4).
7. God's Voice	The Pope speaks to create conformity to the "church."	The Bible speaks, we give mental and cognitive assent, and nothing new is created.	God speaks to us because Jesus' sheep hear His voice and His words are creative.
8. Teaching and Doctrine	Teaching is church dogma/doctrine, and may be informed by church tradition.	Teaching is the theology of my denomination.	Teaching is both the body of doctrine and learning to hear God's voice and obey it (that is, faith).
9. Prophecy	The Pope (and some historical saints) can speak prophetically.	No one receives revelation and prophecy any longer. All miracles, revelation, and prophecy have ceased. (Westminster Confession 1:1)	Prophecy is the central gift to anyone in the new covenant (Isa.59:21 > Acts 2:39; Jer. 31:34 > 2 Cor. 3).
10. God's Voice and Revelation	Church tradition reveals God's thoughts.	Systematic theology reveals God's thoughts.	Revelation gifts reveal God's thoughts, usually with a "now" context.
11. Who Can Hear God?	The Pope hears from God for us.	The pastor hears from God for us through Bible study.	We hear from God through His voice in our hearts, which is the essence of the new covenant (Jer. 31:34; Isa. 59:21 > Acts 2:39).

Issue	Catholic Abuses	Protestant Reaction	Jesus' Model
12. Tradition vs. Authoritative Revelation	The church adds traditions, which may or may not conform to biblical norms.	The church adds rules, which may or may not conform to biblical norms.	God's voice clarifies everything (i.e., "But I say unto you…").
13. Theology vs. Revelation	Emphasis on theology codified by the church	Emphasis on theology codified by the denomination	Emphasis on revelation within believer's heart, as against "scribal religion" (John 5:36-43)
14. Ministry Genesis	Parishioners support the church programs.	Church members support the church programs.	Believers minister based on leading via the prophetic Spirit and meet the needs of individuals they meet.
15. Repentance of Sin	Uses "confessional" to repent of sin.	Uses altar calls to repent of sin	The focus is on the Spirit's overcoming power in whatever context.
16. Baptism	Baptism at birth	Baptism at birth and/or new birth	Numerous baptisms: water, Spirit, fire, and into the body of Christ
17. Church Emphasis	Focus is the building of the church structure and programs.	Focus is to get people saved.	Focus is to manifest the kingdom of God.
18. Discipleship	Making disciples is training them in church doctrine and right living.	Making disciples is training them in church doctrine and right living.	Making disciples is training them to live by the power and voice of the Holy Spirit in addition to sound doctrine and right living.
19. The Nature of Knowledge and Revelation	Detached propositional knowledge concerning church	Detached propositional knowledge concerning Bible	Revelation-based learning from the Holy Spirit

Issue	Catholic Abuses	Protestant Reaction	Jesus' Model
20. Leadership Development	Training from pulpit and classroom	Training from pulpit and classroom	Apprenticeship: on-the-road modeling, experience
21. Structure	Structure is rows of pews in church buildings; focus on the Eucharist and the altar.	Structure is rows of pews in church buildings; focus on the pulpit and the preacher.	Structure is one-on-one and circles in home meetings, perhaps in addition to the two items above.
22. Church Discipline	Church must control with threat of excommunication.	Denomination must control with threat of excommunication (and revocation of property).	Believers use the gifts to seek repentance and reconciliation with one another, guided by love (1 Cor. 14:1).

APPENDIX D

Unbelief

THE PROBLEM OF unbelief in the church can hardly be over-stated. We absolutely struggle to believe that God can and will do anything due to the onslaught of false teaching (often from the media and universities, but sometimes from the church itself), the absence of clear-cut examples of victory, and a lack of biblical knowledge (even in the church) about the ways and power of God. (See again Matthew 22:29.)

As it pertains to healing, one Scripture confounds us. Even when we read it and acknowledge it, we gloss over the depth of its implications. Mark 6:5–6 says: "And He could do no miracle there, except that He laid His hand on a few sick people and healed them. And He wondered at their unbelief."

Unbelief is the great diffuser and dissipater of God's power. I'm talking about societal, institutional, and generational unbelief that codifies itself and holds an entire populace captive, then relent-lessly infects their minds like some kind of virus. This is some-thing I often refer to as "matrixed unbelief," and it's the kind we find ourselves up against most often in the West. *Even Jesus* could not withstand this kind of unbelief; when facing it, the power released from Him was reduced until all He could do was heal a few sick people. He was astonished at the level of unbelief he encountered in Nazareth; the whole community was steeped in it.

Similarly, Western civilization—Australian, American, European, and beyond—has the same problem. Moreover, it is getting worse. Jesus predicted this, saying, "Hear what the unrigh-teous judge said; now, will not God bring about justice for His elect who cry to Him day and night, and will He delay long over them?" [The correct answer appears to be, "Yes, God will bring about justice, and no He will not delay long." If something in that answer takes our breath away, that shows how deeply the virus of the age has laid hold of our thinking and our faith.] "Nevertheless, when the Son of Man comes, will He find faith on the earth" (Luke 18:8, mev)?

This is the question of the hour. When Jesus comes—to our homes, to our churches, to our schools, to our hospitals—is He welcomed with genuine expectant faith or is He hindered because we as a society have marginalized Him, just as His own countrymen in Nazareth did?

The father of the demonized boy in Mark 9:24 cried out to Jesus, "I believe; help my unbelief!" Did the father say that because he was desperate for his son? Yes, but he was also responding to this challenge to his unbelief: "Jesus said to him, 'If you can'! *All things are possible* for one *who believes*" (Mark 9:23, emphasis added). Now *that* is a radical statement, and it has been dumbed down, watered down, and made of no effect because we fear becoming "too extreme." Yet even so, Jesus responded to this man's desire for greater belief by strengthening him with a demonstration of His power.

I don't know how far this current move of the Spirit can or will go, but I do know this: the longer it goes, the more I believe, and the more I believe, the more amazing and powerful things I see. Maybe these Scriptures need to be brought into the light and re-examined. Maybe they contain the nuclear fuel we need to see the power of God unleashed upon the world and upon us.

Just before the Mark 9 incident, Jesus issued a strange warning to his disciples. He told them, "Watch out; beware of the leaven of the Pharisees and the leaven of Herod" (Mark 8:15). Apparently, this was a significant risk. Otherwise, He would not have said, "Watch out!" The disciples were neither Pharisees nor part of

Herod's court, yet there was something about both the religious spirit of the Pharisees and the political spirit of Herod that had the capacity to work its way through every part of their lives, just like leaven (yeast) could do with dough. This "leaven" was a dangerous, corrupting influence. But the disciples didn't get it. They began discussing their lack of bread among themselves until Jesus rebuked them for being clueless to the fact that bread had nothing to do with it. (See Mark 8:16–17.)

Their problem in fact was that their hearts were becoming dull and insensitive to the very things they were living among, the things of the Spirit that they were seeing *every day*. These things were just as plainly set before the Pharisees and Herod Antipas, but they refused to see. Instead, Herod and the Pharisees had intense animosity toward Jesus—as had Herod the Great, who sought to destroy Him in infancy, questioning His work, and doubting His mission, even actively seeking Jesus' torture and death. They were the ones who resisted the kingdom of God and sought to manipulate God's anointing as though it were merely tricks and parlor games. Yet Jesus said the mentality of these two groups could infect *them*—His disciples!

Please understand that I am not writing this in an accusatory way, but in a reflective, meditative way. I am still thinking and praying about the matter of unbelief and how to address it in myself, but I think the father in Mark 9 was onto something. He cried out that he believed, but he needed help with his unbelief. This attitude of the heart includes recognizing that we are all susceptible to the corrupting influence of self-seeking outward religious displays and self-serving political behaviors that breed unbelief. The people who are trapped by these influences are the ones who start out uncomfortable with the work of God and ultimately seek to stop it altogether.

Do we need sound doctrine and sound practice? Certainly, we do. Should we honor the position of those in spiritual authority?

Yes! Despite all I've written, Jesus ascribes to the Pharisees the authority to "[sit] on Moses' seat" (Matt. 23:2). When the Word and the Spirit become separated, however, a grave danger lurks. I fear that we have become infected with the leaven of the Pharisees and of Herod. The question before us is, "Now that we know it is there, will we plead with Jesus to help us get it out?"

Notes

PILLAR 1

1. *Seeking the Divine: Journey of the Soul*, PDFCOOKIE, https://pdfcookie.com/documents/seeking-the-divine-wrvr79r8p42o?.
2. *Seeking the Divine.*
3. *Seeking the Divine.*
4. *Seeking the Divine.*
5. *Seeking the Divine.*

PILLAR 4

1. *Dictionary.com*, s.v. "strive," accessed February 7, 2023, https://www.dictionary.com/browse/strive.
2. William P. Merrill, "Rise Up, O Men of God!," Timeless Truths, 1911, https://library.timelesstruths.org/music/Rise_Up_O_Men_of_God/.

PILLAR 5

1. *The NAS New Testament Greek*, s.v. "*homothumadon,*" accessed February 7, 2023, https://www.biblestudytools.com/lexicons/greek/nas/homothumadon.html.
2. People who have this most commonly have Germanic or Austrian roots. It's not exclusive to those countries, but it's common there. There are also French people with it; Denmark and Norway came under Nazi control. Those with Nazi spirits will have had a direct ancestor who belonged to the Nazi Party or was an active participant. If they are honest, they'll have some sort of odd feeling about people who are not Aryan (Caucasian with blond hair and blue eyes). They may not openly espouse such beliefs, but in their hearts they are thinking, "I don't want my kid

dating someone like that," and so on. In the presence of the Holy Spirit, they may actually do the *Seig Heil* salute.

I ran into it in Uganda one time in a person working with refugees who had had a curse put on him by a witch doctor. As we were finishing up, I said, "Is there a Nazi spirit here? If so, come to the surface." And *bam!* There it was.

Another time, two men disrupted a meeting I was leading in Wolfsburg, Austria—the birthplace of the National Socialist Party. The first guy stood up and did the salute. I told him to sit down and he didn't. As this open power encounter was taking place in front of the whole congregation, another guy on the other side of the room did the same. I told them both to sit down and that I was not playing around. Neither one did. So I said, "OK, in Jesus' name, *come out!*" They both did a double backflip over the chairs and the spirits came out. Those men were direct descendants of the men who were in the hotel the day the Nazi Party was formed, and they were carrying that demonic spirit.

A similar thing goes on with the Ku Klux Klan. There's a pretty tight link between that and the Nazis anyway. So we drive it out everywhere we find it. Those spirits are just nasty. The stuff they say, the way they react—I do not like any of that stuff at all. It makes me firm and stern with those demons.

I've also driven many Marxist spirits out of people. They're not the same as Nazi spirits but are just as bad. I'm waiting for my first person who's been down the road with BLM and Antifa to come my way, so I can talk about that.

APPENDIX B

1. Stephen Knight, *The Brotherhood* (Briarcliff Manor, NY: Stein and Day, 1984), 236.

APPENDIX C

1. Jon Mark Ruthven, PhD, *How Jesus Defined Christianity* (Lee's Summit, MO: Christos Publishing, 2023), 143; Mark Virkler, "What's Wrong With Protestant Theology's Foundations?," Communion With God Ministries, accessed February 15, 2023, https://www.cwgministries.org/blogs/protestants-foundations-were-forged-reactions-abuses-catholic-church#.Y-yM7v3f2m4.gmail.

About the Author

KEN FISH IS the founder of Orbis Ministries and a widely regarded expert in prophecy, healing, and deliverance. He travels extensively, teaching on topics that also include spiritual formation, leadership development, and church growth and governance.

He graduated from Princeton University with a degree in history and philosophy of religion before earning a Master of Divinity from Fuller Theological Seminary. He also holds an MBA in finance and strategy from UCLA's Anderson Graduate School of Management.

Fish spent more than twenty-five years as a senior executive with Fortune 500 companies. Additionally, he has served as an adviser to political leaders in several nations. Since 2010, Fish's work has included vision casting for spiritual awakening and equipping people to embrace their life's calling as Christians. This work has taken him to over forty-five nations on six continents.

Fish has been a repeat guest on various media outlets such as the Trinity Broadcasting Network, *The Eric Metaxas Radio Show*, *Premier Christianity* magazine, and MorningStarTV's *Prophetic Perspectives on Current Events*. He and his wife, Beth, have three adult children and live in the Los Angeles area.